The Merrill Studies
in
The Scarlet Letter

Compiled by

Arlin Turner
Duke University

Charles E. Merrill Publishing Company
A Bell & Howell Company
Columbus, Ohio

CHARLES E. MERRILL STUDIES

Under the General Editorship of
Matthew J. Bruccoli and Joseph Katz

ISBN: 0-675-09319-8

Library of Congress Catalog Number: 76-120276

1 2 3 4 5 6 7 8 9 10 — 79 78 77 76 75 74 73 72 71 70

Printed in the United States of America

Preface

To make a collection of significant writings on *The Scarlet Letter* is to choose selections among our major literary critics and scholars. Hawthorne's works, and especially his finest novel, have invited the attention of our most perceptive interpreters to themes, characters, and narrative techniques, and to the mind and the literary views of the author.

In reporting the steps in Hawthorne's planning and writing of *The Scarlet Letter*, James T. Fields, his friend and publisher, provides such intimate details as we have for perhaps no other major literary work. The essay by Hubert H. Hoeltje supplements Fields's account by setting down what is known about the circumstances under which the book was written. Hawthorne's preface to the second edition is his own statement on the circumstance which had drawn most comment, his dismissal from the Salem Custom House. Charles Ryskamp does more than fill in the historical background for *The Scarlet Letter;* he explores Hawthorne's attitudes toward Puritan New England and his methods of employing history for his fictional purposes.

Reviewers of *The Scarlet Letter* in 1850 touched on most of the elements that have attracted later comment, and some of them showed acute perception of Hawthorne's special qualities. Evert A. Duyckinck called the book a psychological romance, "a drama in which thoughts are acts." E. P. Whipple noted how "purely objective" Hawthorne is in the treatment of his characters; he valued "The Custom House" because it is "instinct with the vital spirit of humor." The reviewers knew of Hawthorne's dismissal from the

Custom House and had sympathy to offer, but George Ripley found "too sharp touches of the caustic acid" in the sketch. Henry F. Chorley, writing from England, found *The Scarlet Letter* a "mixture of Puritan reserve and wild imagination, of passion and description, of the allegorical and the real." He was not sure the elements of the plot are proper for fiction, but he could find no fault with the treatment in the book. A strong indictment on moral grounds was written by Arthur Cleveland Coxe for the *Church Review* of January, 1851 (not included in the present volume).

In the half century after Hawthorne, the realistic novelists valued him, learned from him, and used his fiction as a bench-mark from which to measure and to control their variations from his practice. Anthony Trollope compares his works directly with Hawthorne's; Henry James says less in direct comparison, but his comment on Hawthorne's works conveys equally important indirect comment on his own works. What James or any other major novelist may say about himself while looking at Hawthorne is likely to be a significant criticism of Hawthorne.

The extensive and specialized study of Hawthorne which dates from about 1930 has produced far more good essays on *The Scarlet Letter* than can be printed in this volume. The selections have been made to represent different approaches, divergent interpretations, and varying emphases; but especially they have been made to furnish help to an understanding and an appreciation of one of the greatest American novels.

A. T.

Contents

4. Revival and Reassessment

1. Origins and Composition

James T. Fields

[The Reluctant Author of
The Scarlet Letter]

When Mr. George Bancroft, then Collector of the Port of Boston, appointed Hawthorne weigher and gauger in the custom-house, he did a wise thing, for no public officer ever performed his disagreeable duties better than our romancer. Here is a tattered little official document signed by Hawthorne when he was watching over the interests of the country: it certifies his attendance at the unlading of a brig, then lying at Long Wharf in Boston. I keep this precious relic side by side with one of a similar custom-house character, signed *Robert Burns*.

I came to know Hawthorne very intimately after the Whigs displaced the Democratic romancer from office. In my ardent desire to have him retained in the public service, his salary at that time being his sole dependence, — not foreseeing that his withdrawal from that sort of employment would be the best thing for American letters that could possibly happen, — I called, in his behalf, on several influential politicians of the day, and well remember the rebuffs I received in my enthusiasm for the author of the "Twice-Told Tales." One pompous little gentleman in authority, after

From *Yesterdays with Authors* (Boston, 1871), pp. 48–52.

hearing my appeal, quite astounded me by his ignorance of the claims of a literary man on his country. "Yes, yes," he sarcastically croaked down his public turtle-fed throat, "I see through it all, I see through it; this Hawthorne is one of them 'ere visionists, and we don't want no such a man as him round." So the "visionist" was not allowed to remain in office, and the country was better served by him in another way. In the winter of 1849, after he had been ejected from the custom-house, I went down to Salem to see him and inquire after his health, for we heard he had been suffering from illness. He was then living in a modest wooden house in Mall Street, if I remember rightly the location. I found him alone in a chamber over the sitting-room of the dwelling; and as the day was cold, he was hovering near a stove. We fell into talk about his future prospects, and he was, as I feared I should find him, in a very desponding mood. "Now," said I, "is the time for you to publish, for I know during these years in Salem you must have got something ready for the press." "Nonsense," said he; "what heart had I to write anything, when my publishers (M. and Company) have been so many years trying to sell a small edition of the 'Twice-Told Tales'?" I still pressed upon him the good chances he would have now with something new. "Who would risk publishing a book for *me*, the most unpopular writer in America?" "I would," said I, "and would start with an edition of two thousand copies of anything you write." "What madness!" he exclaimed; "your friendship for me gets the better of your judgment. No, no," he continued; "I have no money to indemnify a publisher's losses on my account." I looked at my watch and found that the train would soon be starting for Boston, and I knew there was not much time to lose in trying to discover what had been his literary work during these last few years in Salem. I remember that I pressed him to reveal to me what he had been writing. He shook his head and gave me to understand he had produced nothing. At that moment I caught sight of a bureau or set of drawers near where we were sitting; and immediately it occurred to me that hidden away somewhere in that article of furniture was a story or stories by the author of the "Twice-Told Tales," and I became so positive of it that I charged him vehemently with the fact. He seemed surprised, I thought, but shook his head again; and I rose to take my leave, begging him not to come into the cold entry, saying I would come back and see him again in a few days. I was hurrying down the stairs when he called after me from the chamber, asking me to stop a moment. Then quickly stepping into the entry with a roll of manuscript in his hands, he said: "How in Heaven's name did you know this thing was there? As you have found me out, take what I have written, and tell me, after you get home and have time to read it, if it is good for anything. It is either very good or very bad, — I don't know which." On my way up to Boston I read the germ of "The Scarlet Letter"; before I slept that night I wrote him a note all aglow with admiration of the marvellous story he had put into my hands, and told him that I would come again to Salem the next day and arrange for its publication. I went on in such an amazing state of excitement when we met again in the little house, that he would not believe I was really in earnest. He seemed to think I was beside myself, and laughed sadly at my enthusiasm. However, we soon arranged for his appearance again before the public with a book.

This quarto volume before me contains numerous letters, written by him from 1850 down to the month of his death. The first one refers to "The Scarlet Letter," and is dated in January, 1850. At my suggestion he had altered the plan of that story. It was his intention to make "The Scarlet Letter" one of several short stories, all to be included in one volume, and to be called

OLD-TIME LEGENDS:
TOGETHER WITH SKETCHES,
EXPERIMENTAL AND IDEAL.

His first design was to make "The Scarlet Letter" occupy about two hundred pages in his new book; but I persuaded him, after reading the first chapters of the story, to elaborate it, and publish it as a separate work. After it was settled that "The Scarlet Letter" should be enlarged and printed by itself in a volume he wrote to me: —

I am truly glad that you like the Introduction, for I was rather afraid that it might appear absurd and impertinent to be talking about myself, when nobody, that I know of, has requested any information on that subject.

As regards the size of the book, I have been thinking a good deal about it. Considered merely as a matter of taste and beauty, the form of publication which you recommend seems to me much preferable to that of the "Mosses."

In the present case, however, I have some doubts of the expediency, because, if the book is made up entirely of "The Scarlet Letter," it will be too sombre. I found it impossible to relieve the shadows of the story with so much light as I would gladly have thrown in. Keeping so close to its point as the tale does, and diversified no otherwise than by turning different sides of the same dark idea to the reader's eye, it will weary very many people and disgust some. Is it safe, then, to stake the fate of the book entirely on this one chance? A hunter loads his gun with a bullet and several buckshot; and, following his sagacious example, it was my purpose to conjoin the one long story with half a dozen shorter ones, so that, failing to kill the public outright with my biggest and heaviest lump of lead, I might have other chances with the smaller bits, individually and in the aggregate. However, I am willing to leave these considerations to your judgment, and should not be sorry to have you decide for the separate publication.

In this latter event it appears to me that the only proper title for the book would be "The Scarlet Letter," for "The Custom-House" is merely introductory, — an entrance-hall to the magnificent edifice which I throw open to my guests. It would be funny if, seeing the further passages so dark and dismal, they should all choose to stop there! If "The Scarlet Letter" is to be the title, would it not be well to print it on the title-page in red ink? I am not quite sure about the good taste of so doing, but it would certainly be piquant and appropriate, and, I think, attractive to the great gull whom we are endeavoring to circumvent.

Hubert H. Hoeltje

The Writing of
The Scarlet Letter

The Paradise which Nathaniel Hawthorne and his wife Sophia had found within the walls of the Old Manse in Concord during their honeymoon was presently invaded by a progressively uncomfortable poverty. The magazines for which he wrote were seemingly paying less than ever for fiction, and their payments were increasingly slow. He found it embarrassing, in the village of Concord, that he could not pay his household bills. He could not even afford to buy paper for his writing. When Sophia had gone to visit her parents, he wrote to her that he was going to bed at dark to save the cost of oil for his lamp. Sophia, for her part, observed that all their clothing seemed to be wearing out at once. It became necessary, at last, to borrow money from his college friend Horatio Bridge.

These embarrassments were the more irksome as they became the subject of public gossip. When Hawthorne returned for a visit to his native Salem, he learned that the most pitiable stories about his poverty had been told by Charles W. Upham, who, not long before, had been in Concord, and returned to Salem with an

From *The New England Quarterly,* XXVII (September 1954), 326-346. Reprinted by permission of the publisher and H. H. Hoeltje, Jr.

account which almost made it appear that Hawthorne and his wife were actually suffering for lack of food, and that a government office was Hawthorne's only alternative of the almshouse. Though Hawthorne did not wish to be considered wealthier than he was, he did not think himself quite a pauper, and was irked to find himself represented as such.[1] For Upham, who for twenty years had been a pastor of the First Church of Salem, Hawthorne was to retain a long suspicion and dislike. Indeed, if Hawthorne was ever to have an enemy, Upham was to be the man, though, in 1844, when all this happened, the romancer was yet to learn how far political ambition may lead its victim. Now, when Hawthorne erroneously assumed that he had learned, through his Boston Custom House experience, to know a politician, Upham had not yet entered politics, and Hawthorne thought of him only as a disagreeable gossip. At the moment, this experience merely added gall to the bitterness of Hawthorne's poverty. It was perhaps the more disagreeable because it was true, as Upham may have known, that Hawthorne was seeking a government office.

Indeed, ever since his employment in the Boston Custom House Hawthorne had entertained hopes of obtaining a government position, though he wished for something more congenial than work in the holds of merchant ships. For a number of years the postmastership at Salem seemed to dangle almost within his reach, though at last that hope gave way to more realizable possibilities. At any rate, from the time of his marriage and during the period of his residence in the Old Manse at Concord, his diary and his letters—to his sister Louisa and his friends Bridge and Hillard, among others — reveal the never-ceasing expectation of a government station which would do away with the necessity of writing for bread. In fact, in a letter to Sophia in which he had told of the stories that Upham had scattered in Salem, Hawthorne had written of Bridge's efforts in Washington to help forward his official enterprises.

It was Bridge who invited Hawthorne and Sophia and Una to spend two weeks at his bachelor quarters at the Navy Yard near Portsmouth, New Hampshire, where other guests were former Senator and Mrs. Pierce, Senator and Mrs. Atherton of New Hampshire, and Senator Fairfield of Maine. Bridge's purpose in having Hawthorne meet these influential people was attained before

---

[1] *Love Letters of Nathaniel Hawthorne, 1839-41 and 1841-63* (Chicago, 1907), II, 118.

the close of autumn, for by that time all had used their influence
with President Polk and Secretary of the Treasury Walker in
behalf of a government position for Hawthorne.[2]

Nor were other friends less active. Early in January of the
following year, the distinguished Charles Sumner wrote to Mrs.
George Bancroft to intercede with her husband for Hawthorne.
Hawthorne, wrote Sumner, was "very poor indeed"; besides, he
was "a genius," "an ornament of the country," whose appointment
to a government position would delight all, regardless of party.
To this letter Bancroft, now Acting Secretary of War under President Polk, replied that he was glad that Sumner went for the good
rule of dismissing wicked Whigs and putting in Democrats. "Set
me down as without influence," wrote Bancroft, "if so soon as the
course of business will properly permit, you do not find Hawthorne
an office holder."[3] And in another area of activity Hawthorne had
the aid of another friend, John L. O'Sullivan, editor of *The Democratic Review,* to which Hawthorne contributed numerous tales
and sketches later gathered together into *Twice-Told Tales* and
Mosses from an Old Manse. O'Sullivan had written that something
would be done for Hawthorne. "For the purpose of presenting you
more advantageously," wrote O'Sullivan, "I have got Duyckinck
to write an article about you in the April *Democratic;* and what is
more, I want your consent to sit for a daguerreotype, that I may
take your head off in it. Or, if Sophia prefers, could she not make
a drawing based on a daguerreotype? By manufacturing you thus
into a Personage, I want to raise your mark higher in Polk's
appreciation."[4] If after such efforts in his behalf Hawthorne was
to fail of his aim, clearly it was not for want of friends. Sophia,
in writing to her mother, had expressed the truth, as was her
custom, ecstatically: "How his friends do love him!"

Meanwhile, as these movements were being directed toward
Washington and the President, there was no less activity in his
cause in Hawthorne's native Salem. In mid-autumn of 1845 the
local Democratic organizations, as well as individuals prominent
locally, gathered their forces to obtain for Hawthorne the Surveyorship of the Port of Salem. The series of petitions addressed to
President Polk began with a letter from the District Committee

---

[2]Horatio Bridge, *Personal Recollections of Nathaniel Hawthorne* (New York,
1893), 108-110.
[3]M. A. DeWolfe Howe, editor, *Life and Letters of George Bancroft* (New York,
1908), I, 264-267.
[4]Julian Hawthorne, *Nathaniel Hawthorne and His Wife* (Boston, 1885), I, 285.

of the Second Congressional District of Massachusetts, penned and signed by its chairman, H. L. Conolly. There was a letter, also, from the Town Committee of the Democratic Party of Salem, signed by all seven of its members, including, once more, H. L. Conolly. Finally, there was a letter from the Essex County Committee. And in addition to these solicitations there were communications from the publishers of *The Salem Advertiser*, local Democratic newspaper, and Benjamin F. Browne, postmaster of Salem. Hawthorne could scarcely have wished for a more complete — or an apparently more enthusiastic — support.

Presumably, to be effective, letters of recommendation must point out the merits of the candidate, and since the basis of Hawthorne's candidacy was later to become a subject of cruel contention, it may be interesting to glance at the contents of the letters themselves. The party had selected Hawthorne, in the first place, because he was a Democrat, and so his party allegiance was indicated. Hawthorne, said the letter from *The Salem Advertiser*, had always been "a pure and primitive Democrat in principle"; and Senator Fairfield wrote likewise that Hawthorne had always been "a Democrat in principle, feeling and action," but added, "though never a warm partisan." There was at least equal if not greater emphasis in Fairfield's letter on Hawthorne's literary reputation and personal character. "For purity and elegance of style," wrote Fairfield, "if not for originality and force, he has no superior, in my opinion, among our best writers. He is a man of great purity of character — and is warmly and extensively beloved." Pierce said nothing of Hawthorne's party affiliation, and remarked only that Hawthorne was a personal friend, a genius, and "a most excellent and honorable man." Senator Atherton's letter stressed no partisanship: "Mr. Hawthorne is an honor to the Literature of the Country, a man of unblemished reputation and high sense of honor, and his appointment to the office for which he is proposed would gratify many others besides the Democracy of New England." Since Sumner was a prominent Whig, his approval could not have been inspired by political bias. It will be remembered that he pleaded Hawthorne's need and his genius. "Nor is there a person of any party," he had written, "who would not hear of his appointment with delight."[5]

---

[5]These items pertaining to Hawthorne's candidacy, as well as those mentioned later regarding his discharge, including the "Memorial," are to be found in the files of the Treasury Department, Washington, D. C.

There were months of uncertainty and anxious waiting before the political powers in Washington came to a decision. Meanwhile, the owner of the Old Manse wishing possession, the Hawthornes lived intermittently in Salem and in Boston, while Sophia was expecting her second child. When there was no news about the surveyorship, they consoled themselves with the thought that it was yet too early to hear. In their more hopeful moments, when the prospects of a regular income made the future seem bright, they even had thoughts of building their own home, though Hawthorne feared, after all, that it was only a castle in the air. Nevertheless, as he wrote to Sophia on one of the numerous occasions when they were separated, "a moderate smile of Providence would cause it to spring out of the earth, on that beautiful hillside, like a flower in the summer time. With a cottage of our own, and the surveyorship, how happy we might be! — happier than in Concord, on many accounts." Then, with an admixture of disappointment with confidence, he added: "The Surveyorship I think we shall have, but the cottage implies an extra thousand or fifteen hundred dollars." Late in February, O'Sullivan wrote that the President had promised to favor Hawthorne. Almost at the same time, Wiley and Putnam announced that they were about to publish two volumes of Hawthorne's tales, *Mosses from an Old Manse*. Things were beginning to look up. On March 23, there was a letter from Senator Fairfield announcing that the President had named Hawthorne Surveyor of the Salem Custom House. The salary was to be twelve hundred dollars a year—enough so that Hawthorne would no longer be compelled to write to earn bread, something that seemed to him, just then, the most unprofitable business in the world![6]

There were, however, difficulties. With two children, it was not easy to find a place to live; hence they stayed for a time with Hawthorne's mother and sisters on Herbert Street, and Sophia was often in Boston, where Julian was born. At last they found an upstairs apartment on Chestnut Street, where Una enjoyed the birds that visited the trees there, though there was no place for her to play. It was almost two years before they found a house (at $200 a year) on Mall Street, near the Common. It had the advantage of being near the Custom House, and, more importantly, of having on the third floor, near the street, a study, high above all noise, where Hawthorne retired to write in the afternoons when he was free from his duties as surveyor. For a year, Sophia said, he had lived in the

[6]*Love Letters,* II, 159-160; J. H., 309.

nursery, without solitude, without an opportunity to muse, and without his desk being once opened.

It was, indeed, with his own children and in his own home, that Hawthorne found his greatest happiness during these years. If the routine of the surveyorship irked, or if his pen failed him in his study, there yet remained his afternoons and evenings with his family. Six years of marriage had not dulled his sentiments. Now that he had shelter and clothes, and daily bread, without the anguish of debt pressing upon him continually, he was as contented as one could hope to be. It hardly seemed possible that he and Sophia could be the parents of these children. He was most sensible of the wonder, and the mystery, and the happiness. When they and their mother were in Boston, where Sophia's parents lived, he rambled about the house and permitted the play of his feelings when he chanced to see some garment of Sophia's, or any of the playthings of the children. He counted the days, the hours almost, when they should return. And Sophia, on her part, was no less happy. Not every mother had such a father for her children. Even when both children were screaming at once, she said, she was no less sensible of her happiness than when both were making the most dulcet of sounds. No art or beauty, she wrote to her mother, could excel her daily life, with such a husband and such children. Small wonder, then, that when his family was gone, even for a short visit, the time was a miserable one for Hawthorne. They were sunless days. The house was melancholy. It chilled his heart. When all were together, however, the days and the years melted rapidly away. Their present life had hardly substance and tangibility enough — the future too soon became the present, which, before they could grasp it, looked back upon them as the past.[7]

While these dreamlike years were thus vanishing so swiftly, a sufficiently gross tangibility was drawing nearer to Hawthorne's affairs after a fashion that he scarcely imagined, through events that seemed, for a time, to have no relation to his own life. On the seventh day of June, 1848, the Whig party, at its national convention in Philadelphia, nominated General Zachary Taylor, "Old Rough and Ready," hero of the Mexican War. The uniqueness of that convention lay in the fact that it was a convention without a platform. The Whigs chose rather to run their candidate on the

---

[7]*Love Letters,* II, 173-204; *passim;* Rose Hawthorne Lathrop, *Memories of Hawthorne* (Boston, 1897), 88-89; Randall Stewart, editor, *The American Notebooks by Nathaniel Hawthorne* (New Haven, 1932), 197.

broad basis of a pre-convention statement which the General had
made in his so-called "Allison Letter." Perhaps it was a sincere
statement, made by a man of forthright character but inexperi-
enced in the devious ways of politics, a statement serving as the
best of battle cries for those skilled in turning the words of an art-
less man to party uses. If Hawthorne saw Taylor's letter when it
first appeared in the public press (he was to see it many time before
he was done with Salem), it must have reassured him, if he thought
of it as affecting him at all. "I have no private purpose to accom-
plish," protested the General, "no party objects to build up, no
enemies to punish—nothing to serve but my country. . . . I reiterate
what I have so often said — I am a Whig. If elected, I would not be
the mere President of a party. I would endeavor to act independent
of all party denomination. I should feel bound to administer the
Government untrammeled by party schemes." [8]

It seemed clear enough. Proscription for party reasons, which
Andrew Jackson had practised with such apparent violence, was to
cease. So mild a politician as Hawthorne, "never a warm partisan,"
surely need have no fear of such magnanimity and patriotism. But
whatever Hawthorne thought of Taylor's assurance, he was presently to learn that, translated into the language and action of the
local politician, they were to be put to quite practical party uses. In
Salem, where Hawthorne was directly concerned, they were used
in an astonishing fashion. There, in mid-August, Charles W. Upham
was elected to the presidency of the local Taylor Club, and upon
that occasion, in addressing the club, illustrated a political talent
later to be used devastatingly against Hawthorne himself.

Upham, a brilliant student while at Harvard, where he was a
classmate of Ralph Waldo Emerson, was already a man of promi-
nence in Salem. He was to live and die a First Citizen, though not
without some skeptics among those who knew him. While Upham
was mayor of Salem, a contemporary wrote of him mischievously:
". . . there was never a Mayor more efficient and at the same time
delighted with his office and *power*; everything and every man feels
it; even the dust heaps in the street sneak away when he approaches. His style of meeting 'the people' is grand, majestic, con-
descending, cordial, dignified and popular at once." Longfellow
described him in his journal as a "fat, red, rowdy chap, with only
a twinkle of talent in his eye, and no lambent light playing over

---

[8]Oliver Otis Howard, *General Taylor* (New York, 1912), 306-320, *passim.*

the whole countenance, as truly refined and intellectual men generally have." Charles Sumner spoke of him as "that smooth, smiling, oily man of God." Hawthorne came to regard him as "the most satisfactory villain that ever was . . . at every point . . . consummate." But that was later — after Upham had done his worst with Hawthorne, and when Hawthorne was contemplating revenge.[9]

It was because General Taylor had declared the sentiments expressed in the Allison Letter, said Upham in his address to the Taylor Club, that the General was such a favorite. By the choice of Taylor as candidate, the Whig party had "given evidence that it is not held together, nor stimulated to action, by the prospect of the spoils of office. It has higher objects than the advancement of emolument of individuals." But from such lofty impartiality Upham descended, in his next breath, to practical politics. "General Taylor," he went on to say, "will undoubtedly surround himself with a cabinet of Whigs—of eminent men who shall have proved, by their course in the election, that they concur with him in his own individual principles. He will take care to do justice to his friends in the exercise of his patronage, as occasion shall arise"; and then, to turn the thought back to its original height, he added, "but in his general administration, he will be the President, not of a party, but of the people — treating with paternal and impartial kindness all sections, all interests, and all persons."[10] However General Taylor regarded patronage before he came into office, Upham had made it clear that there was to be no nonsense, after a Whig victory, in retaining Democrats in local appointive offices.

Meanwhile, in the quiet of his home on Mall Street, Hawthorne may have been oblivious to the activities of Upham and the Taylor Club. Even at the Custom House on sleepy Derby wharf he may have thought himself far from the rush of the whirlpool of political vicissitude. But as he whiled away his mornings in his cobwebbed office, lounging on his long-legged stool before his old pine desk, his eyes wandering up and down the columns of the morning newspaper, he must have been aware, as *The Salem Gazette* asserted, that the Whigs were "awake." Even on remote Mall Street there must have echoed some blare of horns and roar of voices as the Whigs for miles around — from as far as Boston — rallied in Salem

---

[9]"Letters Written by Dr. Ernest Bruno von de Gersdorff to Hon. Stephen Palfrey Webb, 1849-55," *Essex Institute Historical Collections,* LXXIX, 143; Stewart, 288; R. H. L., 100-101.

[10]*Salem* (Mass.) *Gazette,* Aug. 22, 1848.

on a September night to hear the eloquent Rufus Choate, in a campaign speech, praise that "plain, brave old man who had filled the measure of his country's glory." And after the Taylor victory in November, no one in Salem could have been unaware of the Great Jubilee to celebrate the new era — when there would be no more President-made wars for the extension of slavery, no more tariffs to injure northern interests, no more kingly usurpations and abuses of veto power, and no more corrupt and corrupting use of official patronage. So said the Whigs.[11]

How very much awake the Whigs were, and what reforms in official patronage they would introduce, were matters soon made clear. On the very day of the great Jubilee, Hawthorne's friend, Benjamin Browne, having had enough experience in politics to see the handwriting on the wall, resigned as postmaster of Salem. On the very day following the inauguration of "Old Rough and Ready," the rumblings of a threat to dismiss Hawthorne himself from his surveyorship were so near at hand that Hawthorne wrote a frightened letter to his Whig friend in Boston, Attorney George S. Hillard, asking for his aid in Whig circles should the threat draw nearer. On June second, a local Salem paper announced twenty-four new appointments to subordinate places in the custom house of the neighboring city of Boston, an example of the exercise of the Whig pledge of "no proscription." On June eighth Hawthorne received a telegram from Washington peremptorily announcing his dismissal. On the following day the news of the dismissal was made public by the press.[12]

Precisely how Hawthorne's discharge was effected, or who was directly responsible for initiating the action, no longer remains a matter of extant record, though the files of the Treasury Department at Washington, D. C., contain many documents pertaining to the later features of this famous case. As the question was explained to Hawthorne by some loyal Whig friends (and Hawthorne had many friends among the Whigs), his discharge was the answer to a petition drawn up by Charles W. Upham and signed by some thirty citizens of Salem. The one accusation in the petition which came to Hawthorne's ears—the one upon which the discharge was apparently based—was plainly false: namely, that Hawthorne had

---

[11]*Salem Gazette,* Sept. 29, and Nov. 18, 1848.
[12]*Salem Gazette,* Nov. 17, 1848; Moncure D. Conway, *Life of Nathaniel Hawthorne* (London, undated), 111; *Salem Gazette,* June 2, 1849; R. H. L., 93.

been active in "Locofoco" politics antagonistic to the election of General Taylor. An atmosphere of secrecy surrounds this petition. The intention seems to have been to strike surreptitiously and quickly before the victim could defend himself.[13]

The ruse, however clever, could not long remain secret. If, as it appears, it was the aim of Upham and the petitioners to effect the removal of the surveyor before the administration at Washington was aware that it was *the* Hawthorne who was being displaced, it was not long before Washington was apprised of what had been done. Indeed, on the very day when Hawthorne's dismissal was made public, a letter of protest was addressed to the Secretary of the Treasury by no less eminent a Whig than Rufus Choate, who had sung the praises of that "plain, brave old man" now so soon breaking his pre-election promises of "no proscription." Other prominent Whigs, including the scholar and historian George Ticknor, joined in the remonstrance. It was a matter of concern to these men that their party should show so little regard for a literary genius such as Hawthorne, and should lay itself open to the flood of criticism sure to follow.

The earliest of the letters could hardly have reached Washington before the criticism began. The newspapers raised a storm which raged from Washington to New England and which rolled to the distant banks of the Mississippi and the new country of the West before it was spent. For a month the discharge of Hawthorne from the surveyorship at Salem received prominent position in the news columns and editorials of city and county newspapers alike. Zachary Taylor's dismissal of Nathaniel Hawthorne became a sensation of the day.

Representative of the newspaper criticism which joined the names of the President of the United States and the author of *Twice-Told Tales* was an editorial in *The New York Evening Post,* edited by William Cullen Bryant, long famous as the author of "Thanatopsis" and now one of the outstanding journalistic forces in the country. "If General Taylor," said this editorial, "was pledged to any principle of policy, he was pledged against removals from office for opinion's sake. A more flagrant violation of that pledge cannot be imagined, than is exhibited in the removal of Mr. Hawthorne. . . . His removal was an act of wanton and

---

[13]Letters from Amory Holbrook, Salem, Mass., June 20, 1849, in the Treasury files; R. H. L., 95-97.

unmitigated oppression; but worse than that, it was, or seems to have been, a gross breach of public faith on the part of the President."

Whatever had originally been said by the Salem Whigs to obtain Hawthorne's dismissal, their defense, when first the secret was out, was based on political grounds, quite ignoring the pre-election claims that General Taylor would remove no appointee for political opinions, but only for inefficiency or dishonesty. A Salem writer in *The Boston Atlas* (June 16, 1849) summarized the Whig case against Hawthorne by stating that the latter had obtained his original appointment solely on account of his Locofocoism. Oblivious to his own contradictions, this writer maintained that Hawthorne had never received the approval of the local Salem Democrats, though he had served actively on Town and State Democratic committees. Hawthorne's political activities were further revealed, wrote this anonymous writer, by his contributions to *The Democratic Review* and the Salem Democratic newspapers, and by walking in the Locofoco torch-light processions.

Within the week following the publication of the *Atlas* article Hawthorne himself replied in a cogent letter addressed to his Whig friend in Boston, Hillard, who had long been prominent in Whig circles in Massachusetts. Hillard had the influence necessary to obtain the publication of this letter in *The Boston Advertiser* (June 21, 1849), a leading Whig journal, and thus helped his friend deal a cutting blow to his Salem enemies. Hawthorne's reply was the clearest and manliest of statements, and his marshalling of the evidence made the falsity of all the charges manifest and ludicrous. How Hawthorne was appointed to the surveyorship, and the relative emphasis of his literary reputation and his political activity in obtaining that appointment, has already been told in these paragraphs. His contributions to the Salem Democratic newspaper, *The Register*, and to *The Democratic Review*, were literary in character, as might easily be ascertained. As for walking in torch-light processions, he assured his accusers, not without some humor, he would hardly have done anything so little in accordance with his tastes and character had the result of the Presidential election depended upon it.

The force of Hawthorne's letter, together with the hue and cry of protest against the discharge which appeared in Whig and Democratic newspapers alike, was not without its effect. The Administration at Washington temporarily withheld the appointment of Hawthorne's successor in the surveyorship, and the Salem Whigs, fearful that their ends would be defeated, took a new tack. Since it was only too apparent that they had acted in contradiction to General Taylor's campaign slogan of "no proscription," they now took a course more consistent with the President's protestations; that is, they now charged Hawthorne with "corruption, iniquity and fraud" in his capacity as a federal officer. The public press being largely hostile to their efforts, and friendly to Hawthorne's cause, they chose to bring pressure to bear directly upon the Administration. Preparations were therefore made to address a memorial to Secretary of the Treasury William M. Meredith. Unquestionably, in spite of his public avowals of friendship for Hawthorne, the prime mover in this action was Charles W. Upham, recently resigned from the ministry and now embarked upon a political career marked, in years to come, by considerable success. How far Upham and his coadjutors were willing to go to gain their political ends is illustrated by a letter to Meredith informing him of their new "testimony." Co-signers of this letter with Upham were Nathaniel Silsbee, Jr., son of Senator Silsbee, and at various times mayor of Salem, representative in the Massachusetts legislature, and treasurer of Harvard University; and N. B. Mansfield, shipping merchant of Salem, and seemingly a lesser light in the community. It would be their aim, said the signers of this letter (dated June 25, 1849), to show the corruption in the Salem Custom House, a corruption "countenanced, helped out and supported by all the talents which Mr. Hawthorne may have possessed."

Other letters to Meredith followed — a bombardment of them: from Upham; from John Chapman, editor of the Whig *Salem Register*, a long letter foreshadowing the tenuousness of the later "Memorial" itself; and from Daniel P. King, Representative to Congress from Massachusetts. A number of Salem Whigs journeyed to Washington for personal interviews with Meredith. These actions, together with others that followed, indicate the determination — and perhaps the desperation — with which Hawthorne was being hounded. They also indicate the strength of the local forces arrayed against him.

The promised Memorial was in preparation for a fortnight, needfully so because it was a complex document. Its writing was preceded by a number of meetings of the Whig Ward Committee and the Taylor Club. Present at these meetings to oust Hawthorne were, among others, some who had been friends of his in happier days. There, for instance, was the renegade Conolly, now turned

Whig and engaged, as Hawthorne was to say later, in "stabbing him in the back"; there, too, sadly and bitterly for Hawthorne if he knew, was Caleb Foote, in whose *Salem Gazette* some of Hawthorne's first tales and sketches had appeared, who had once predicted for his young townsman a wide and enduring fame, and to whose wife ("Dear, sweet, tender, loving Mary") Sophia had once written intimate, friendly letters picturing the idyllic life at Concord.[14] There, also, apparently, or serving on one of the committees appointed at these meetings, was Richard S. Rogers, a Salem merchant and politician whose name appears in these records but once or twice, but whom Hawthorne later chose to immortalize in his incomparable fantasy, "Feathertop," in which the leading figure is a man of straw, with an unreckonable amount of wealth, a great deal of brass, a fair outside, and a personality so completely and consummately artificial as to be a work of art. And there, moreover, was Charles W. Upham, who submitted the Memorial itself.

It must have cost Upham many an hour to compose that Memorial, which is still extant in its fifteen pages of carefully written longhand. It is an interesting document — startling, exasperating, and — today — amusing. What labor it must have required — the effort to harmonize such a hodgepodge of truth, half-truth, misunderstanding, and misrepresentation! It is nearly a work of art — if, indeed, its ultimate success does not argue its artistry. Upham, brother-in-law of Oliver Wendell Holmes, and later celebrated as the author of a book on Salem witchcraft, had not without reason stood second in his class at Harvard. Small wonder that Hawthorne contemplated doing his best to kill and scalp him in the public prints. Fortunately, however, he was to make far better use of him as Judge Pyncheon in *The House of the Seven Gables*, where the Judge now stands as one of the most satisfactory villains in American literature.

The Memorial proposed to tell the whole story of Hawthorne's ousting. The writer protests, in spite of his own speech before the Taylor Club a year previous, that the Whigs, upon the election of General Taylor, had no thought of requesting a change of officers in the local Custom House. In the very next paragraph, however, he confesses that they took such changes for granted, thus, too,

---

[14]*Salem Gazette,* March 14 and 17, 1837; R. H. L., 55. Regrettably, Foote apparently left no record of his early and friendly relations with Hawthorne, though he had published "The Hollow of the Three Hills" and other pieces of Hawthorne's writings. See Mary Wilder Tileston, editor, *Caleb and Mary Wilder Foote, Reminiscences and Letters* (Boston, 1918).

quite ignoring the pre-election slogan of "no proscription." When no changes were forthcoming, said the Memorial, and when it appeared that Hawthorne was even being protected by his superior in the Custom House, himself a Whig, it became evident that there could be no removal of any Democrats until Hawthorne was first displaced.

To obtain their "rightful authority over the Custom House," therefore, said Upham, they were obliged to eliminate the man placed as a barrier in their way. For this purpose they brought forth the Blue Book, by which they purported to show "one of the most flagrant instances of political financiering, and official extortion and corruption yet developed." More particularly, they sought to show that under Hawthorne gross favoritism had been shown to the Democratic at the expense of the Whig employees in the Custom House. (This was the "corruption" which had been "countenanced, helped out and supported by all the talents which Mr. Hawthorne may have possessed.") What made Hawthorne the more culpable was the fact that one of the men affected was poor, made dependent by a family of eleven children!

Having thus made it appear that Hawthorne was guilty of "corruption, iniquity and fraud," Upham went on, in the conclusion of the Memorial, to assure the Administration that Hawthorne was nevertheless to a great extent the abused instrument of others. He spoke of Hawthorne's "true manliness of character," of how his friends should rejoice that he was to be removed from influences and connections so uncongenial to him, and of how greatly the Whigs of his native city appreciated his reputation as "one of the most amiable and eloquent writers of America"—none more, indeed, than they!

How baseless all these declarations were is perhaps best shown, not by Hawthorne's forthright letters to his brother-in-law, Horace Mann, Whig Representative to Congress from Massachusetts, who sought to aid him, but by the words of Upham himself. Whatever it was necessary to say in a formal document such as the Memorial, at home in Salem everybody who read *The Register* knew Upham's intents. In an interview with a representative of that newspaper (probably the editor, John Chapman himself) Upham made it clear that "Mr. Hawthorne's removal had become necessary to vindicate the authority of the Whigs of Salem." As manifesting his own disbelief in the charges of "corruption, iniquity and fraud," or in the small relevance of such matters in public office-holding, Upham represented himself, with characteristic protestation of friendship, as seeking, in government service, an even better position for Hawthorne elsewhere![15]

Nevertheless, the Memorial effected its ends. Within the month, on July 24, 1849, Hawthorne's successor to the surveyorship received his official appointment. Nor were the charges against Hawthorne ever withdrawn. Never, within his lifetime, was he cleared of the accusations so unjustly but so successfully fabricated. Officially, the stigma remained.

In the midst of this country-wide publicity, and while his adversaries were still deep in their intrigue, Hawthorne was trying as bravely as he could to face the world once more without an income. Sophia, according to the oft-told story, greeted the first news of his dismissal with the remark, "Oh, then, you can write your book!" But actually the dismissal dragged on for the greater part of two months, during which he was never quite certain what the outcome would be. It was a distressing period. Little by little, however, the necessity for writing once more took possession of him, not only because his family needs and the haunting memories of his former poverty drove him on, but also, as he said in a letter to Conolly, because he wished to put his enemies to blush.[16] What he seems to have had in mind was another volume of tales and sketches, which he intended to call *Old-Time Legends*, a book somewhat after the fashion of *Twice-Told Tales* and *Mosses from an Old Manse*.

These plans, however, were not easily realized. Even as Hawthorne learned of his final dismissal, he was beset by another adversity that made writing a heavy if not impossible task. His mother, who was living with his two sisters in separate quarters in the rambling house on Mall Street, became seriously ill and suffered the most intense pains. It was a shocking experience to see the alterations in her appearance as the agonizing days crept on. One day, as he stood by the bedside of his dying mother, through a crevice of the curtain he saw his little daughter Una playing in the yard, a beautiful child with golden locks, and so full of life that she seemed life itself. In the contrast, the whole of human existence appeared to be revealed at once. What a mockery if this were all of life, whatever the measure of happiness between the extremes! There must be something beyond, or life would be an insult as well as a wrong, to end in this miserable way. So he comforted himself

---

[15]J. H., II, 379-385; *Salem Register*, June 25, 1849.
[16]Lenox, Mass., July 15, 1850; quoted in *The Boston Globe*, July 3, 1904.

with the assurance of a better state of being, though he confessed that it was surely the darkest hour that he had ever lived.[17]

After the death of his mother, the need for money became more and more acute. His salary had been small, and since he had come to the surveyorship in debt, the family savings were soon gone. In his need, he accepted aid from his friends — Hillard and others — though it was a bitter experience to do so. He was deeply ashamed, because he was convinced that the fault of failure is in a great degree attributable to the man who fails. In the circumstances, he could retain his own self-respect only by making the generosity of his friends an incitement to his utmost exertions so that he might not need their help again.[18]

With these spurs to action, the need for money and the wish to justify himself before the world, Hawthorne was presently writing "immensely," as Sophia said, with some fright at her husband's intensity of effort. He had come near a brain fever when his mother lay dying, though now, for a time, he was well again. But before his task was done, his step had lost its usual elasticity, and the vigor of his youth had gone. "His eyes," said Sophia, "looked like two immense spheres of troubled light; his face was wan and shadowy. . . ." It was the most trying year of his life. From the shock and strain of these events he seems never to have recovered fully. Vainly, in later years, he tried to blot from his mind the unhappy memory of this period. The Whigs had won their little victory at Salem at a fearful cost to Hawthorne.[19]

Even after the *Old-Time Legends* were taking shape, there remained Hawthorne's doubt that any publisher would publish his work. The small sale of his two previous volumes made him think of himself as the most unpopular writer in America. When, in this despondency and during this period of illness he was visited by his new-found friend, the publisher James T. Fields, he was reluctant even to show what he had written, uncertain whether it was as good as he hoped or as bad as he feared. When Fields at last persuaded him to let him have such manuscript as he had concealed in his study, Fields was in an amazing state of excitement over what Hawthorne gave him. It was Fields's suggestion, however, that the tale of "The Scarlet Letter" be enlarged and published as a

[17]Stewart, 209-210.
[18]Nathaniel Hawthorne, *The Complete Writings* (Boston, 1900), XVII, 433.
[19]J. H., I, 358, 363; R. H. L., 130; Stewart, 303.

separate work. Before publication, therefore, there remained the difficult and wearisome task of revision and addition.

Finally, however, even this task was accomplished, and *The Scarlet Letter* was finished on February 3, 1850, as Hawthorne wrote the next day to his friend Horatio Bridge. On the very night of its completion he had read the conclusion to Sophia, who had been heartbroken by this tale of human frailty and sorrow, and who had gone to bed with a grievous headache. Hawthorne remembered, in after years, how, as he had tried to read, his voice swelled and heaved, as if he were tossed up and down on an ocean as it subsides in a storm. He remembered, too, the very great nervous state he had been in and the great diversity of emotion he had experienced for many a month.[20]

His fatiguing work completed, Hawthorne prepared to bid farewell forever to the "abominable" city of Salem; for, now that his mother was gone, there was no longer anything to keep him there. Though Fields had spoken of *The Scarlet Letter* in tremendous terms of approbation, Hawthorne himself was by no means confident that his book would obtain a wide popularity. In a quite workaday manner he set about to find a new home in Western Massachusetts to seek relief in the country from the strenuous ordeal of the last few months.[21] *The Scarlet Letter* was what Hawthorne had hardly dared to hope it would be — "a ten-strike." The first edition sold out in little more than a week, and a second edition was quickly printed.[22]

The truth is that neither Hawthorne nor anyone else had foreseen the consequences of the petty political conspiracy which had so unjustly deprived him of his position at the Salem Custom House. It had been a matter of great embarrassment to Hawthorne to see himself "careering through the public prints," and to find it necessary to defend himself in the newspapers against calumny. Sophia, it is true, was aware that her husband's name was "ringing through the land" and that he was finding himself very famous. Hawthorne's old friend O'Sullivan, now no longer publisher of *The Democratic Review*, had really pointed the case when he had written to Washington, after Hawthorne's discharge, that Hawthorne's dismissal was a "national" issue.[23] Nevertheless, none of these truly saw how far-reaching the consequences were to be.

---

[20]Bridge, 110-111; N. H., xix, 370-371.
[21]R. H. L., 108; Bridge, 111-112.
[22]Bridge, 113.
[23]R. H. L., 99; O'Sullivan's letter was dated New York, June 22, 1849.

Quite unexpectedly, the Salem conspiracy was of the greatest advantage to its victim. Throughout the country, newspapers had echoed the indignation of William Cullen Bryant's *New York Evening Post* at the flagrant violation of General Taylor's pledge when Hawthorne had been dismissed. Like *The Evening Post,* too, they had linked the name of Nathaniel Hawthorne with that of the President of the United States — to the advantage, not of the President, but of the humble surveyor and modest author. No writer in the history of American literature had ever received an equal publicity. When *The Scarlet Letter* appeared, its author's name was known wherever newspapers were read. With its publication, Nathaniel Hawthorne was the best-known writer of prose fiction in America. That the book was, after this unprecedented publicity, a great masterpiece of our literature, is one of the fortunate circumstances of history.

One word remains to be added. In those dark days when his enemies were laying before the highest powers in the land charges of "corruption, iniquity and fraud," Hawthorne consoled himself with the assurance that everything was for the best. Then and all his life he was convinced that what seemed to be misfortune proved in the end to be the best that could possibly have happened to him. Upham, Conolly, and the rest, the agents of his adversity, were but a part of an inevitable Providence.[24] Sophia had expressed their common conviction, one beautiful April evening in the early days of their marriage, as they watched the sunset from the windows of the Old Manse: "Man's accidents are God's purposes."

If the reader will visit the Old Manse at Concord, he can still see these words where they were scratched with Sophia's diamond upon the pane of the western window of Hawthorne's study.

---

[24]Bridge, 145; R. H. L., 94-95.

Nathaniel Hawthorne

Preface to the Second Edition
[of *The Scarlet Letter*]

Much to the author's surprise, and (if he may say so without additional offence) considerably to his amusement, he finds that his sketch of official life, introductory to THE SCARLET LETTER, has created an unprecedented excitement in the respectable community immediately around him. It could hardly have been more violent, indeed, had he burned down the Custom House, and quenched its last smoking ember in the blood of a certain venerable personage, against whom he is supposed to cherish a peculiar malevolence. As the public disapprobation would weigh very heavily on him, were he conscious of deserving it, the author begs leave to say that he has carefully read over the introductory pages, with a purpose to alter or expunge whatever might be found amiss, and to make the best reparation in his power for the atrocities of which he has been adjudged guilty. But it appears to him, that the only remarkable features of the sketch are its frank and genuine good-humor, and the general accuracy with which he has conveyed his sincere impressions of the characters therein described. As to enmity, or ill-feeling of any kind, personal or political, he utterly disclaims such

From *The Scarlet Letter* (Boston: Ticknor, Reed, and Fields, 1850), pp. iii-iv.

motives. The sketch might, perhaps, have been wholly omitted, without loss to the public, or detriment to the book; but, having undertaken to write it, he conceives that it could not have been done in a better or a kindlier spirit, nor, so far as his abilities availed, with a livelier effect of truth.

The author is constrained, therefore, to republish his introductory sketch without the change of a word.

SALEM, *March 30, 1850.*

Charles Ryskamp

The New England Sources of
The Scarlet Letter

After all the careful studies of the origins of Hawthorne's tales and the extensive inquiry into the English sources of *The Scarlet Letter*,[1] it is surprising that the American sources for the factual background of his most famous novel have been largely unnoticed. As would seem only natural, Hawthorne used the most creditable history of Boston available to him at that time, and one which is still an important source for the identification of houses of the early settlers and for landmarks in the city. The book is Dr. Caleb H. Snow's *History of Boston*. Study and comparison of the many histories read by Hawthorne reveal his repeated use of it for authentication of the setting of *The Scarlet Letter*. Consequently, for the most part this article will be concerned with Snow's book.

From *American Literature*, XXXI (November 1959), 257-272. Reprinted by permission of the author and Duke University Press.
[1] I shall make no reference to the English sources of *The Scarlet Letter* which have been investigated by Alfred S. Reid in *The Yellow Ruff and The Scarlet Letter* (Gainesville, 1955) and in his edition of *Sir Thomas Overbury's Vision . . . and Other English Sources of Nathaniel Hawthorne's "The Scarlet Letter"* (Gainesville, 1957). Most of this article was written before the publication of Reid's books. It may serve, however, as a complement or corrective to the central thesis put forth by Reid: "that accounts of the murder of Sir Thomas Overbury were Hawthorne's principal sources in composing *The Scarlet Letter*" (*The Yellow Ruff*, p. 112). The page references in my text to *The Scarlet Letter* are to the Riverside edition (Boston, 1883).

If we are to see the accurate background Hawthorne created, some works other than Snow's must also be mentioned, and the structure of time as well as place must be established. Then it will become apparent that although Hawthorne usually demanded authentic details of colonial history, some small changes were necessary in his portrayal of New England in the 1640's. These were not made because of lack of knowledge of the facts, nor merely by whim, but according to definite purposes — so that the plot would develop smoothly to produce the grand and simple balance of the book as we know it.

During the "solitary years," 1825-37, Hawthorne was "deeply engaged in reading everything he could lay his hands on. It was said in those days that he had read every book in the Athenaeum. . . ."[2] Yet no scholar has studied his notebooks without expressing surprise at the exceptionally few remarks there on his reading. Infrequently one will find a bit of "curious information, sometimes with, more often without, a notation of the source; and some of these passages find their way into his creative work."[3] But for the most part Hawthorne did not reveal clues concerning the books he read and used in his own stories. About half of his writings deal in some way with colonial American history, and Professor Turner believes that "Hawthorne's indebtedness to the history of New England was a good deal larger than has ordinarily been supposed."[4] Certainly in *The Scarlet Letter* the indebtedness was much more direct than has hitherto been known.

Any work on the exact sources would have been almost impossible if it had not been for Hawthorne's particular use of the New England annals. Most of these are similar in content. The later historian builds on those preceding, who, in turn, must inevitably base all history on the chronicles, diaries, and records of the first settlers. Occasionally an annalist turns up a hitherto unpublished fact, a new relationship, a fresh description. It is these that Hawthorne seizes upon for his stories, for they would, of course, strike the mind of one who had read almost all the histories, and who was

---

[2]James T. Fields, *Yesterdays with Authors* (Boston, 1900), p. 47. For a list of books which Hawthorne borrowed from the Salem Athenaeum, see Marion L. Kesselring, *Hawthorne's Reading 1828-1850* (New York, 1949). All of my sources are included in this list, except the second edition (1845) of Felt's *Annals of Salem*.

[3]*The American Notebooks,* ed. Randall Stewart (New Haven, 1932), p. xxxii.

[4]H. Arlin Turner, "Hawthorne's Literary Borrowings," *PMLA,* LI, 545 (June, 1936).

intimate with the fundamentals of colonial New England government.

As a young bachelor in Salem Hawthorne, according to his future sister-in-law, Elizabeth Peabody, "made himself thoroughly
acquainted with the ancient history of Salem, and especially with
the witchcraft era."[5] This meant that he studied Increase Mather's
Illustrious Providences and Cotton Mather's *Magnalia Christi
Americana*. He read the local histories of all the important New
England towns. He read—and mentioned in his works—Bancroft's
History of the United States, Hutchinson's *History of Massachusetts*, Snow's *History of Boston*, Felt's *Annals of Salem*, and
Winthrop's *Journal*.[6] His son reported that Hawthorne pored over
the daily records of the past: newspapers, magazines, chronicles,
English state trials, "all manner of lists of things. . . . The forgotten volumes of the New England Annalists were favorites of his,
and he drew not a little material from them."[7] He used these works
to establish verisimilitude and greater materiality for his own
books. His reading was perhaps most often chosen to help him—as
he wrote to Longfellow—"give a life-like semblance to such shadowy stuff"[8] as formed his romances. Basically it was an old method
of achieving reality, most successfully accomplished in his own day
by Scott; but for Hawthorne the ultimate effects were quite different. Here and there Hawthorne reported actual places, incidents,
and people — historical facts — and these were united with the creations of his mind. His explicitly stated aim in *The Scarlet Letter*
was that "the Actual and the Imaginary may meet, and each imbue itself with the nature of the other" (p. 55). His audience
should recognize "the authenticity of the outline" (p. 52) of the
novel, and this would help them to accept the actuality of the
passion and guilt which it contained. For the author himself, the
strongest reality of outline or scene was in the past, especially the
history of New England.

---

[5]Moncure D. Conway, *Life of Nathaniel Hawthorne* (New York, 1890), p. 31.
[6]Edward Dawson, *Hawthorne's Knowledge and Use of New England History:
A Study of Sources* (Nashville, Tenn., 1939), pp. 5-6; Turner, p. 551.
[7]Julian Hawthorne, *Hawthorne Reading* (Cleveland, 1902), pp. 107-108, 111,
132. Hawthorne's sister Elizabeth wrote to James T. Fields: "There was [at
the Athenaeum] also much that related to the early History of New England
. . . . I think if you looked over a file of old Colonial Newspapers you would
not be surprised at the fascination my brother found in them. There were a
few volumes in the Salem Athenaeum; he always complained because there
were no more" (Randall Stewart, "Recollections of Hawthorne by His Sister
Elizabeth," *American Literature*, XVI, 324, 330, Jan., 1945).
[8]*The American Notebooks*, p. xlii.

The time scheme of the plot of *The Scarlet Letter* may be dated definitely. In Chapter XII, "The Minister's Vigil," the event which brings the various characters together is the death of Governor Winthrop. From the records we know that the old magistrate died on March 26, 1649.⁹ However, Hawthorne gives the occasion as Saturday, "an obscure night of early May" (pp. 179, 191). Some suggestions may be made as reasons for changing the date. It would be difficult to have a night-long vigil in the cold, blustery month of March without serious plot complications. The rigidly conceived last chapters of the book require a short period of time to be dramatically and psychologically effective. The mounting tension in the mind and heart of the Reverend Mr. Dimmesdale cries for release, for revelation of his secret sin. Hawthorne realized that for a powerful climax, not more than a week, or two weeks at the most, should elapse between the night of Winthrop's death, when Dimmesdale stood on the scaffold, and the public announcement of his sin to the crowd on Election Day. The Election Day (p. 275) and the Election Sermons (p. 257) were well-known and traditionally established in the early colony in the months of May or June.¹⁰ (The election of 1649, at which John Endicott became governor, was held on May 2.) Consequently Hawthorne was forced to choose between two historical events, more than a month apart. He wisely selected May, rather than March, 1649, for the time of the action of the last half of the book (Chapters XII-XXIII).

⁹William Allen, *An American Biographical and Historical Dictionary* (Cambridge, Mass., 1809), p. 616; Caleb H. Snow, *A History of Boston* (Boston, 1825) p. 104; Thomas Hutchinson, *The History of Massachusetts* (Salem, 1795), I, 142.
¹⁰John Winthrop, *The History of New England from 1630 to 1649* (Boston, 1825-1826), II, 31, 218 (a note on p. 31 states that the charter of 1629 provided for a general election on "the last Wednesday in Easter term yearly"; after 1691, on the last Wednesday of May); also Daniel Neal, *The History of New-England . . . to . . . 1700* (London, 1747), II, 252. Speaking of New England festivals, Neal writes: "their Grand Festivals are the Day of the annual Election of Magistrates at *Boston,* which is the latter End of *May;* and the Commencement at Cambridge, which is the last *Wednesday* in *July,* when Business is pretty much laid aside, and the People are as chearful among their Friends and Neighbors, as the *English* are at *Christmas.*" Note Hawthorne's description of Election Day (*The Scarlet Letter,* p. 275): "Had they followed their hereditary taste, the New England settlers would have illustrated all events of public importance by bonfires, banquets, pageantries and processions . . . . There was some shadow of an attempt of this kind in the mode of celebrating the day on which the political year of the colony commenced. The dim reflection of a remembered splendor, a colorless and manifold diluted repetition of what they had beheld in proud old London . . . might be traced in the customs which our forefathers instituted, with reference to the annual installation of magistrates."

The minister's expiatory watch on the scaffold is just seven years after Hester Prynne first faced the hostile Puritans on the same platform (pp. 179, 194, 205). Therefore, the first four chapters of *The Scarlet Letter* may be placed in June, 1642 (see p. 68). Hawthorne says that at this time Bellingham was governor (pp. 85-86). Again one does not find perfect historical accuracy; if it were so, then Winthrop would have been governor, for Bellingham had finished his term of office just one month before.[11] A possible reason for Hawthorne's choice of Bellingham will be discussed later.

The next major scene—that in which Hester Prynne goes to the mansion of Bellingham — takes place three years later (1645).[12] Hawthorne correctly observes: "though the chances of a popular election had caused this former ruler to descend a step or two from the highest rank, he still held an honorable and influential place among the colonial magistracy" (p. 125).[13] From the description of the garden of Bellingham's house we know that the time of the year was late summer (pp. 132-133).

With these references to time, as Edward Dawson has suggested,[14] we can divide the major action of the novel as follows:

Act One

i. Chapters I-III. The Market-Place, Boston. A June morning, 1642.
ii. Chapter IV. The Prison, Boston. Afternoon of the same day.

Act Two

Chapters VII-VIII. The home of Richard Bellingham, Boston. Late summer, 1645.

Act Three

i. Chapter XII. The Market-Place. Saturday night, early May, 1649.
ii. Chapters XIV-XV. The sea coast, "a retired part of the peninsula" (p. 202). Several days later.
iii. Chapters XVI-XIX. The forest. Several days later.

---

[11]Winthrop, II, 31: June 2, 1641, Richard Bellingham elected governor. Winthrop, II, 63: May 18, 1642, John Winthrop elected governor.
[12]*The Scarlet Letter*, p. 138: "Pearl, therefore, so large were the attainments of her three years' lifetime, could have borne a fair examination in the New England Primer, or the first column of the Westminster Catechisms, although unacquainted with the outward form of either of those celebrated works." The Westminster Catechisms were not formulated until 1647; the New England Primer was first brought out ca. 1690.
[13]Winthrop, II, 220: on May 14, 1645. Thomas Dudley had been elected governor.
[14]I am largely indebted to Dawson, p. 17, for this time scheme.

Act Four

Chapters xxi-xxiii. The Market-Place. Three days later.

The place of each action is just as carefully described as is the time. Hawthorne's picture of Boston is done with precise authenticity. A detailed street-by-street and house-by-house description of the city in 1650 is given by Snow in his *History of Boston*. It is certainly the most complete history of the early days in any work available to Hawthorne. Whether he had an early map of Boston cannot be known but it is doubtful that any existed from the year 1650. However, the City of Boston Records, 1634-1660, and the "Book of Possessions" with the reconstructed maps (made in 1903-1905 by George Lamb, based on the original records) prove conclusively the exactness of the descriptions written by Snow and Hawthorne.

Hawthorne locates the first scene of *The Scarlet Letter* in this way:

> . . . it may safely be assumed that the forefathers of Boston had built the first prison-house somewhere in the vicinity of Cornhill, almost as seasonably as they marked out the first burial-ground, on Isaac Johnson's lot, and round about his grave, which subsequently became the nucleus of all the congregated sepulchres in the old churchyard of King's Chapel. (p. 67)[15]

> It was no great distance, in those days, from the prison-door to the marketplace . . . . Hester Prynne. . . came to a sort of scaffold, at the western extremity of the market-place. It stood nearly beneath the eaves of Boston's earliest church, and appeared to be a fixture there. (pp. 75-76)[16]

---

[15]Concerning Isaac Johnson, Snow writes: "According to his particular desire expressed on his death bed, he was buried at the Southwest corner of the lot, and the people exhibited their attachment to him, by ordering their bodies to be buried near him. This was the origin of the first burying place, at present the Chapel burial ground" (p. 37).

[16]Justin Winsor, in *The Memorial History of Boston* (Boston, 1881), I, 506, 539, writes: "The whipping-post appears as a land-mark in the Boston records in 1639, and the frequent sentences to be whipped must have made the post entirely familiar to the town. It stood in front of the First Church, and was probably thought to be as necessary to good discipline as a police-station now is . . . . The stocks stood sometimes near the whipping-post . . . . And here, at last, before the very door of the sanctuary, perhaps to show that the Church and State went hand-in-hand in precept and penalty, stood the first whipping-post — no unimportant adjunct of Puritan life."

Snow says that in 1650 Governor Bellingham and the Rev. John Wilson lived on one side of the Market-Place and Church Square (Snow, p. 117). Near Spring Lane on the other side of the Square (mentioned by Hawthorne when little Pearl says, "I saw her, the other day, bespatter the Governor himself with water, at the cattle-trough in Spring Lane," p. 164) was the home of Governor Winthrop (Snow, p. 108). All the action of *The Scarlet Letter* set in Boston is thus centered in the heart of the city. This, as Snow takes great pains to point out, was where all the leading townsmen lived. He writes:

> It has been so often repeated that it is now generally believed the north part of the town was at that period the most populous. We are convinced that the idea is erroneous. . . . The book of possessions records the estates of about 250, the number of their houses, barns, gardens, and sometimes the measurement of their lands. It seems to embrace the period from 1640 to 1650, and we conclude, gives us the names of almost, if not quite, all the freemen of Boston. They were settled through the whole length of the main street on both sides. . . . It is evident too, that most of the wealthy and influential characters lived in what is now the centre of the town. We discover only about thirty names of residents north of the creek. (pp. 128-129)

A clear instance of Hawthorne's borrowing a fact from Snow is in the naming of "Master Brackett, the jailer" (p. 92). Few colonial historians mention a jailer in Boston at this time, and if they do, they give his name as Parker. But Snow, alone it would seem, gives this information about Brackett, after writing about the property of John Leverett: "His next neighbor on the south was Richard Parker or Brackett, whose name we find on the colony records as prison keeper so early as 1638. He had '*the market stead*' on the east, the prison yard west, and the meeting house on the south" (Snow, p. 116). This last sentence taken from Snow gives the exact location of the action of the early chapters of *The Scarlet Letter.*

Another example of Hawthorne's use of Snow is shown in the description of Governor Bellingham's house. Here Hawthorne builds a vivid image of the old mansion. He writes of Hester and Pearl:

> Without further adventure, they reached the dwelling of Governor Bellingham. This was a large wooden house, built in a fashion of

which there are specimens still extant in the streets of our older
towns. . . . It had, indeed, a very cheery aspect; the walls being
overspread with a kind of stucco, in which fragments of broken
glass were plentifully intermixed; so that, when the sunshine fell
aslant-wise over the front of the edifice, it glittered and sparkled as
if diamonds had been flung against it by the double handful. . . .
It was further decorated with strange and seemingly cabalistic
figures and diagrams, suitable to the quaint taste of the age, which
had been drawn in the stucco when newly laid on, and had now
grown hard and durable, for the admiration of after times. (pp.
128-129) [17]

There are almost no representations of the first settlers' houses in
the New England annals. But Snow on one occasion does print an
old plate showing an "Ancient building at the corner of Ann-Street
and Market-Square" (p. 166). And he describes the house in a way
which bears a remarkable resemblance to the sketch written by
Hawthorne twenty-five years later:

This, says a description furnished by a friend, is perhaps the only
wooden building now standing in the city to show what was considered elegance of architecture here, a century and a half ago. . . .
The outside is covered with plastering, or what is commonly called
rough-cast. But instead of pebbles, which are generally used at the
present day to make a hard surface on the mortar, broken glass was
used. This glass appears like that of common junk bottles, broken
into pieces of about half an inch diameter. . . . This surface was
also variegated with ornamental squares, diamonds and flowers-
de-luce. (p. 167) [18]

Snow is also the only historian who tells the story of Mrs. Sher-
man's pig in order to bring out its effect upon the early Massachusetts government. [19] Hawthorne, with his characteristic interest
in the unusual fact from the past, refers to this strange incident:

At that epoch of pristine simplicity, however, matters of even slighter
public interest, and of far less intrinsic weight, than the welfare of

---

[17]Hawthorne also accurately noted that Governor Bellingham was "bred a
lawyer" (p. 131). Snow writes of Bellingham: "He was by education a lawyer"
(p. 159).
[18]For a possible source for details concerning the interior of Bellingham's
house, the front door, knocker, etc., see Joseph B. Felt, *Annals of Salem* (2nd
ed.; Salem, 1845), I, 403-406.
[19]Snow, pp. 95-96. Hutchinson, I, 135-136 also refers to the incident, but not
in this particular way.

Hester and her child, were strangely mixed up with the deliberations of legislators and acts of state. The period was hardly, if at all, earlier than that of our story, when a dispute concerning the right of property in a pig not only caused a fierce and bitter contest in the legislative body of the colony, but resulted in an important modification of the framework itself of the legislature. (p. 126)

In his version of the story Snow said that the incident "gave rise to a change also in regard to the Assistants" (p. 95) and that because of the confusion and dissatisfaction over the decision of the court, "provision was made for some cases in which, if the two houses differed, it was agreed that the major vote of the whole should be decisive. This was the origin of our present Senate" (p. 96).

The characters named in *The Scarlet Letter*—other than Hester, Pearl, Chillingworth, and Dimmesdale, for whom we can find no real historical bases—were actual figures in history. The fictional protagonists of the action move and gain their being in part through their realistic meetings with well-known people of colonial Boston. Even the fantastic Pearl grows somewhat more substantial in the light of the legend and story of her primitive world. She is seen, for example, against the silhouette of the earlier Mr. Blackstone. When describing Bellingham's garden Hawthorne relates: "There were a few rose-bushes, however, and a number of apple-trees, probably the descendants of those planted by the Reverend Mr. Blackstone, the first settler of the peninsula; that half-mythological personage, who rides through our early annals, seated on the back of a bull" (p. 133). Snow had said:

By right of previous possession, Mr. Blackstone had a title to proprietorship in the whole peninsula. It was in fact for a time called Blackstone's neck. . . . Mr. Blackstone was a very eccentrick character. He was a man of learning, and had received episcopal ordination in England . . . . It was not very long before Mr. Blackstone found that there might be more than one kind of nonconformity, and was virtually obliged to leave the remainder of his estate here . . . . Let the cause of his removal have been what it may, certain it is that he went and settled by the Pawtucket river . . . . At this his new plantation he lived uninterrupted for many years, and there raised an orchard, the first that ever bore apples in Rhode Island. He had the first of the sort called yellow sweetings, that were ever in the world, and is said to have planted the first orchard in Massachusetts also. . . . Though he was far from agreeing in opinion with Roger Williams, he used frequently to go to Providence to preach the gospel; and to encourage his younger hearers, while he gratified his own benevolent disposition, he would give them of his apples, which were the first they ever saw. It was said that when he grew old and unable to travel on foot, not having any horse, he used to ride on a bull, which he had tamed and tutored to that use. (pp. 50-53)

This account is taken virtually word for word from a series of articles called "The Historical Account of the Planting and Growth of Providence" published in the Providence *Gazette* (January 12 to March 30, 1765).[20] However, Snow adds to this narrative the application to Boston, which would be of special interest to Hawthorne (the phrase, "and is said to have planted the first orchard in Massachusetts also").

The only minor characters that are developed to such an extent that they become in any way memorable figures are Mrs. Hibbins and the Rev. John Wilson. Hawthorne's use of Mrs. Hibbins shows again a precise interest in the byways of Boston history. He describes the costume of the "reputed witch-lady" carefully (pp. 264, 286). He refers to her as "Governor Bellingham's bitter-tempered sister, . . . the same who, a few years later, was executed as a witch" (p. 144). And again, during the minister's vigil, Hawthorne writes that Dimmesdale beheld "at one of the chamber-windows of Governor Bellingham's mansion . . . the appearance of the old magistrate himself. . . . At another window of the same house, moreover, appeared old Mistress Hibbins, the Governor's sister . . ." (p. 181). In Snow's book there is this account of Mrs. Ann Hibbins:

The most remarkable occurrence in the colony in the year 1655 was the trial and condemnation of Mrs. Ann Hibbins of Boston for witchcraft. Her husband, who died July 23, 1654, was an agent for the colony in England, several years one of the assistants, and a merchant of note in the town; but losses in the latter part of his life had reduced his estate, and increased the natural crabbedness of his wife's temper, which made her turbulent and quarrelsome, and brought her under church censures, and at length rendered her so odious to her neighbours as to cause some of them to accuse her of witchcraft. The jury brought her in guilty, but the magistrates refused to accept the verdict; so the cause came to the general court, where the popular clamour prevailed against her, and the

---

[20]These were reprinted in the Massachusetts Historical Society's *Collections,* 2nd Ser., IX, 166-203 (1820).

miserable old lady was condemned and executed in June 1656.
(p. 140)[21]

There seems to be only one source for Hawthorne's reference to
Mrs. Hibbins as Bellingham's sister. That is in a footnote by James
Savage in the 1825 edition of John Winthrop's *History of New
England,* and it was this edition that Hawthorne borrowed from
the Salem Athenaeum.[22] Savage writes that Mrs. Hibbins "suffered
the punishment of death, for the ridiculous crime, the year after
her husband's decease; her brother, Bellingham, not exerting, perhaps, his highest influence for her preservation."[23] Hawthorne leads
the reader to assume that Mrs. Hibbins, nine years before the
death of her husband, is living at the home of her brother. Hawthorne uses this relationship between Bellingham and Mrs. Hibbins
in order to have fewer stage directions and explanations. It helps
him to establish a more realistic unity in the tale. It partially explains the presence of the various people at the Market-Place the
night of the minister's vigil, since Bellingham's house was just
north of the scaffold. It also suggests why Bellingham is the governor chosen for the opening scenes of the novel, to prevent the plot
from becoming encumbered with too many minor figures.

The Reverend John Wilson's description is sympathetically done,
and it is for the most part historically accurate. Hawthorne presents him as "the reverend and famous John Wilson, the eldest
clergyman of Boston, a great scholar, like most of his contempo-
raries in the profession, and withal a man of kind and genial spirit"
(p. 86). Cotton Mather,[24] William Hubbard,[25] and Caleb Snow
testify to his remarkable "compassion for the distressed and . . .
affection for all" (Snow, p. 156). William Allen, in his *American
Biographical and Historical Dictionary,* writes that "Mr. Wilson
was one of the most humble, pious, and benevolent men of the age,
in which he lived. Kind affections and zeal were the prominent
traits in his character. . . . Every one loved him. . . ."[26] Hawthorne,

---

[21]This is almost a literal copy from Hutchinson, I, 173. See also William Hubbard, "A General History of New England," *Massachusetts Historical Society
Collections,* 2nd Ser., V, 574 (1815); Winthrop, I, 321.
[22]Kesselring, p. 64.
[23]Winthrop, I, 321 n. This contradicts Julian Hawthorne's observation: "As
for Mistress Hibbins, history describes her as Bellingham's relative but does
not say that she was his sister, as is stated in the 'Romance'" ("Scenes of
Hawthorne's Romances," *Century Magazine,* XXVIII, 391, July, 1884).
[24]*Magnalia Christi Americana* (London, 1702), bk. III, p. 46.
[25]Hubbard, p. 604.
[26]Allen, p. 613. The Reverend John Wilson was born in 1588; he died in 1667.

to gain dramatic opposition to Dimmesdale, makes the preacher seem older than he really was. He pictures the man of fifty-seven as "the venerable pastor, John Wilson . . . [with a] beard, white as a snowdrift" (p. 134); and later, as the "good old minister" (p. 182).

Hawthorne's description of Puritan costuming has been substantiated by twentieth-century research. Although the elders of the colonial church dressed in "sad-colored garments, and gray, steeple-crowned hats" (p. 67)[27] and preached simplicity of dress, Hawthorne recognized that "the church attendants never followed that preaching."[28] "Lists of Apparell" left by the old colonists in their wills, inventories of estates, ships' bills of lading, laws telling what must *not* be worn, ministers' sermons denouncing excessive ornamentation in dress, and portraits of the leaders prove that "little of the extreme Puritan is found in the dress of the first Boston colonists."[29] Alice Morse Earle, after going over the lists of clothing brought by the Puritans, concludes:

> From all this cheerful and ample dress, this might well be a Cavalier emigration; in truth, the apparel supplied as an outfit to the Virginia planters (who are generally supposed to be far more given to rich dress) is not as full nor as costly as this apparel of Massachusetts Bay. In this as in every comparison I make, I find little to indicate any difference between Puritan and Cavalier in quantity of garments, in quality, or cost—or, indeed, in form. The differences in England were much exaggerated in print; in America they often existed wholly in men's notions of what a Puritan must be. (I, 34)

Hawthorne's descriptions agree with the early annals. The embroideries and bright colors worn by Pearl, the silks and velvets of Mrs. Hibbins, Hester's needlework — the laces, "deep ruffs . . . and gorgeously embroidered gloves"—were, as he said, "readily allowed

---

[27]The phrase, "steeple-crowned hats," is used by Hawthorne each time he describes the dress of the Puritan elders (*The Scarlet Letter,* pp. 24, 67, 79, 278). The only source that I have been able to find for this particular phrase is in an essay on hats in a series of articles on clothing worn in former times: Joseph Moser, "Vestiges, Collected and Recollected, Number XXIV," *European Magazine,* XLV, 409-415 (1804). The Charge-Books of the Salem Athenaeum show that Hawthorne read the magazine in which this article appeared. Moser wrote about the "elevated and solemn beavers of the Puritans" (p. 414) and the "high and steeple-crowned hats, probably from an idea, that the conjunction of Church and State was necessary to exalt their archetype in the manner that it was exalted" (p. 411).
[28]Alice Morse Earle, *Two Centuries of Costume in America* (New York, 1903), I, 8.
[29]Earle, I, 13.

to individuals dignified by rank or wealth, even while sumptuary laws forbade these and similar extravagances to the plebeian order" (pp. 105-106). The Court in 1651 had recorded "its utter detestation and dislike that men or women of mean condition should take upon them the garb of Gentlemen, by wearing gold or silver lace... which, though allowable to persons of greater Estates or more liberal Education, yet we cannot but judge it intolerable in persons of such like condition."[30] Hawthorne's attempt to create an authentic picture of the seventeenth century is shown in *The American Notebooks* where he describes the "Dress of an old woman, 1656."[31] But all of Hawthorne's description is significant beyond the demands of verisimilitude. In *The Scarlet Letter* he is repeating the impressions which are characteristic of his tales: the portrayal of color contrasts for symbolic purposes, the play of light and dark, the rich color of red against black, the brilliant embroideries[32] on the sable background of the "sad-colored garments."

So far there has been slight mention of the influence of Cotton Mather's writings on *The Scarlet Letter*. These surely require our attention in any study such as this one. Professor Turner believes that certain elements of Mather's *Magnalia Christi Americana*, "and in particular the accounts of God's judgment on adulterers [in II, 397-398], may also have influenced *The Scarlet Letter*. Mather relates [II, 404-405] that a woman who had killed her illegitimate child was exhorted by John Wilson and John Cotton to repent while she was in prison awaiting execution. In like manner, as will be recalled, John Wilson joins with Governor Bellingham and Arthur Dimmesdale in admonishing Hester Prynne to reveal the father of her child."[33] It is possible that an echo of the witch tradition in the *Magnalia Christi Americana* may also be found in *The Scarlet Letter*. "The proposal by Mistress Hibbins that Hester accompany her to a witch meeting is typical of the Mather witch tradition, which included, in accordance with the well known passage in *The Scarlet Letter*, the signing in the devil's book with an iron

---

[30]Winsor, I, 484-485. Hawthorne had read the *Acts and Laws ... of the Massachusetts-Bay in New-England* (Boston, 1726)—see Kesselring, p. 56.

[31]*The American Notebooks*, p. 109.

[32]One of Hawthorne's favorite words—for example, see *The American Notebooks*, p. 97.

[33]Turner, p. 550; Turner is using the Hartford (1855) edition of the *Magnalia Christi Americana*. See *The Scarlet Letter*, pp. 86-91.

pen and with blood for ink. . . . "[34] The Black Man mentioned so often by Hawthorne (pp. 100, 144, 222-225) was familiar to the Puritan settlers of New England. Pearl tells her mother "a story about the Black Man. . . . How he haunts this forest, and carries a book with him, — a big, heavy book, with iron clasps; and how this ugly Black Man offers his book and an iron pen to everybody that meets him here among the trees; and they are to write their names with their own blood" (p. 222). Concerning the Black Man, Cotton Mather had written: "These *Tormentors* tendred unto the afflicted a *Book*, requiring them to *Sign* it, or *Touch* it at least, in token of their consenting to be Listed in the Service of the *Devil;* which they refusing to do, the *Spectres* under the Command of that *Blackman*, as they called him, would apply themselves to Torture them with prodigious Molestations."[35]

Even the portent in the sky, the great red letter A, which was seen on the night of the revered John Winthrop's death (and Dimmesdale's vigil), would not have seemed too strange to Puritan historians. To them it would certainly not have been merely an indication of Hawthorne's gothic interests. Snow had related that when John Cotton had died on Thursday, December 23, 1652, "strange and alarming signs appeared in the heavens, while his body lay, according to the custom of the times, till the Tuesday following" (p. 133).

The idea of the scarlet A had been in Hawthorne's mind for some years before he wrote the novel. In 1844 he had made this comment in his notebooks as a suggestion for a story: "The life of a woman, who, by the old colony law, was condemned always to wear the letter A, sewed on her garment, in token of her having committed adultery."[36] Before that, in "Endicott and the Red Cross," he had told of a "woman with no mean share of beauty" who wore a scarlet A. It has commonly been accepted that the "old colony law" which he had referred to in his notebooks had been

---

[34]Turner, p. 546—see *The Scarlet Letter,* pp. 143-144, and *Magnalia Christi Americana,* bk. VI, p. 81: "It was not long before *M. L.* . . . confess'd that *She* rode with her Mother to the said Witch-meeting . . . . At another time *M. L. junior,* the Grand-daughter, aged about 17 Years . . . declares that . . . they . . . rode on a Stick or Pole in the *Air* . . . and that they set their Hands to the Devil's Book . . . ."
[35]*Magnalia Christi Americana,* bk. II, p. 60; see also Massachussets Historical Society *Collections,* V, 64 (1708); Neal, II, 131, 133-135, 144, 150, 158, 160, 169.
[36]*The American Notebooks,* p. 107.

found in Felt's *Annals of Salem*, where we read under the date of May 5, 1694: "Among such laws, passed this session, were two against Adultery and Polygamy. Those guilty of the first crime, were to sit an hour on the gallows, with ropes about their necks, — be severely whipt not above 40 stripes; and forever after wear a capital A, two inches long, cut out of cloth coloured differently from their clothes, and sewed on the arms, or back parts of their garments so as always to be seen when they were about."[37]

Exactly when Hawthorne began writing *The Scarlet Letter* is not known, but by September 27, 1849, he was working on it throughout every day. It was finished by February 3, 1850.[38] In the novel there is the same rapid skill at composition which is typical of the notebooks. From the multitude of historical facts he knew he could call forth with severe economy only a few to support the scenes of passion or punishment. Perhaps it does not seem good judgment to claim that Hawthorne wrote *The Scarlet Letter* with a copy of Snow's *History of Boston* on the desk. But it does not appear believable that all these incidental facts from New England histories, the exacting time scheme, the authentic description of Boston in the 1640's, should have remained so extremely clear and perfect in his mind when he was under the extraordinary strain of writing the story. Here the studies of Hawthorne's literary borrowings made by Dawson, Turner, and others must be taken into account. They have shown that in certain of his tales, he "seems to have written with his original open before him."[39] To claim a firm dependence upon certain New England histories for the background of *The Scarlet Letter* should therefore not seem unreasonable.

The incidents, places, and persons noticed in this article are the principal New England historical references in *The Scarlet Letter*. A study like this of Hawthorne's sources shows something of his thorough method of reading; it reveals especially his certain knowledge of colonial history and his interest in the unusual, obscure fact. But these are side lights of an author's mind. His steady determination was to make the romances of his imagination as real as the prison-house and the grave.

It would be unfair to leave the study of Hawthorne's historical approach here. His final concern in history was the attempt to find

---

[37]Joseph B. Felt, *The Annals of Salem, from Its First Settlement* (Salem, 1827), p. 317.
[38]Randall Stewart, *Nathaniel Hawthorne* (New Haven, 1948), pp. 93-95.
[39]Turner, p. 547.

the "spiritual significance"[40] of the facts. As his sister Elizabeth had said of the young man: "He was not very fond of history in general."[41] Hawthorne stated concretely his conception of history and the novel in a review (1846) of W. G. Simms's *Views and Reviews in American History:*

> ... we cannot help feeling that the real treasures of his subject have escaped the author's notice. The themes suggested by him, viewed as he views them, would produce nothing but historical novels, cast in the same worn out mould that has been in use these thirty years, and which it is time to break up and fling away. To be the prophet of Art requires almost as high a gift as to be a fulfiller of the prophecy. Mr. Simms has not this gift; he possesses nothing of the magic touch that should cause new intellectual and moral shapes to spring up in the reader's mind, peopling with varied life what had hitherto been a barren waste.[42]

With the evocation of the spirit of the colonial past, and with a realistic embodiment of scene, Hawthorne repeopled a landscape wherein new intellectual and moral shapes could dwell. The new fiction of Hester Prynne and the old appearances of Mrs. Hibbins could not be separated. Time past and time present became explicable as they were identified in the same profound moral engagement.

---

[40]Julian Hawthorne, *Hawthorne Reading*, p. 100.
[41]"Recollections of Hawthorne by His Sister Elizabeth," p. 324.
[42]Stewart, "Hawthorne's Contributions to *The Salem Advertiser*," *American Literature* v, 331-332 (Jan., 1934).

2. The Reception in 1850

[*Evert A. Duyckinck*]

Review of *The Scarlet Letter*

Mr. Hawthorne introduces his new story to the public, the longest of all that he has yet published, and most worthy in this way to be called a romance, with one of those pleasant personal descriptions which are the most charming of his compositions, and of which we had so happy an example in the preface to his last collection, the Mosses from an Old Manse. In these narratives everything seems to fall happily into its place. The style is simple and flowing, the observation accurate and acute; persons and things are represented in their minutest shades, and difficult traits of character presented with an instinct which art might be proud to imitate. They are, in fine, little cabinet pictures exquisitely painted. The readers of the Twice Told Tales will know the pictures to which we allude. They have not, we are sure, forgotten Little Annie's Ramble, or the Sights from a Steeple. This is the Hawthorne of the present day in the sunshine. There is another Hawthorne less companionable, of sterner Puritan aspect, with the shadow of the past over him, a reviver of witchcrafts and of those dark

From the New York *Literary World,* VI (March 30, 1850), 323-325.

agencies of evil which lurk in the human soul, and which even now represent the old gloomy historic era in the microcosm and eternity of the individual; and this Hawthorne is called to mind by such tales as the Minister's Black Veil or the Old Maid in the Winding Sheet, and reappears in the Scarlet Letter, a romance. Romantic in sooth! Such romance as you may read in the intensest sermons of old Puritan divines, or in the mouldy pages of that Marrow of Divinity, the ascetic Jeremy Taylor.

The Scarlet Letter is a psychological romance. The hardiest Mrs. Malaprop would never venture to call it a novel. It is a tale of remorse, a study of character in which the human heart is anatomized, carefully, elaborately, and with striking poetic and dramatic power. Its incidents are simply these. A woman in the early days of Boston becomes the subject of the discipline of the court of those times, and is condemned to stand in the pillory and wear henceforth, in token of her shame, the scarlet letter A attached to her bosom. She carries her child with her to the pillory. Its other parent is unknown. At this opening scene her husband from whom she had been separated in Europe, preceding him by ship across the Atlantic, reappears from the forest, whither he had been thrown by shipwreck on his arrival. He was a man of cold intellectual temperament, and devotes his life thereafter to search for his wife's guilty partner and a fiendish revenge. The young clergyman of the town, a man of a devout sensibility and warmth of heart, is the victim, as this Mephistophilean old physician fixes himself by his side to watch over him and protect his health, an object of great solicitude to his parishioners, and, in reality, to detect his suspected secret and gloat over his tortures. This slow, cool, devilish purpose, like the concoction of some sublimated hell broth, is perfected gradually and inevitably. The wayward, elfish child, a concentration of guilt and passion, binds the interests of the parties together, but throws little sunshine over the scene. These are all the characters, with some casual introductions of the grim personages and manners of the period, unless we add the scarlet letter, which, in Hawthorne's hands, skilled to these allegorical, typical semblances, becomes vitalized as the rest. It is the hero of the volume. The denouement is the death of the clergyman on a day of public festivity, after a public confession in the arms of the pilloried, branded woman. But few as are these main incidents thus briefly told, the action of the story, or its passion, is "long, obscure, and infinite." It is a drama in which thoughts are acts. The material has been thoroughly fused in the writer's mind, and springs forth an entire, perfect creation. We know of no American tales except some of the early ones of Mr. Dana, which approach it in conscientious completeness. Nothing is slurred over, superfluous, or defective. The story is grouped in scenes simply arranged, but with artistic power, yet without any of those painful impressions which the use of the words, as it is the fashion to use them, "grouping" and "artistic" excite, suggesting artifice and effort at the expense of nature and ease.

Mr. Hawthorne has, in fine, shown extraordinary power in this volume, great feeling and discrimination, a subtle knowledge of character in its secret springs and outer manifestations. He blends, too, a delicate fancy with this metaphysical insight. We would instance the chapter towards the close, entitled "The Minister in a Maze," where the effects of a diabolic temptation are curiously depicted, or "The Minister's Vigil," the night scene in the pillory. The atmosphere of the piece also is perfect. It has the mystic element, the weird forest influences of the old Puritan discipline and era. Yet there is no affrightment which belongs purely to history, which has not its echo even in the unlike and perversely commonplace custom-house of Salem. Then for the moral. Though severe, it is wholesome, and is a sounder bit of Puritan divinity than we have been of late accustomed to hear from the degenerate successors of Cotton Mather. We hardly know another writer who has lived so much among the new school who would have handled this delicate subject without an infusion of George Sand. The spirit of his old Puritan ancestors, to whom he refers in the preface, lives in Nathaniel Hawthorne.

We will not mar the integrity of the Scarlet Letter by quoting detached passages. Its simple and perfect unity forbids this. Hardly will the introductory sketch bear this treatment without exposing the writer to some false impressions; but as evidence of the possession of a style faithfully and humorously reflective of the scenes of the passing hour, which we earnestly wish he may pursue in future volumes, we may give one or two separable sketches.

There is a fine, natural portrait of General Miller, the collector; equal in its way to the Old Inspector, the self-sufficing gourmand lately presented in our journal; and there are other officials as well done. A page, however, of as general application, and of as sound profit as any in this office-seeking age, is that which details, in its mental bearing,

THE PARALYSIS OF OFFICE. . . .

The personal situation of Nathaniel Hawthorne — in whom the city by his removal lost an indifferent official, and the world regained a good author — is amusingly presented in this memoir of

A DECAPITATED SURVEYOR. . . .

And a literary man long may he remain, an honor and a support to the craft, of genuine worth and fidelity, to whom no word is idle, no sentiment insincere. Our literature has given to the world no truer product of the American soil, though of a peculiar culture, than Nathaniel Hawthorne.

[Edwin Percy Whipple]

Review of *The Scarlet Letter*

In this beautiful and touching romance Hawthorne has produced something really worthy of the fine and deep genius which lies within him. The "Twice Told Tales," and "Mosses from an Old Manse," are composed simply of sketches and stories, and although such sketches and stories as few living men could write, they are rather indications of the possibilities of his mind than realizations of its native power, penetration, and creativeness. In "The Scarlet Letter" we have a complete work, evincing a true artist's certainty of touch and expression in the exhibition of characters and events, and a keen-sighted and far-sighted vision into the essence and purpose of spiritual laws. There is a profound philosophy underlying the story which will escape many of the readers whose attention is engrossed by the narrative.

The book is prefaced by some fifty pages of autobiographical matter, relating to the author, his native city of Salem, and the Custom House, from which he was ousted by the Whigs. These pages, instinct with the vital spirit of humor, show how rich and exhaustless a fountain of mirth Hawthorne has at his command.

From *Graham's Magazine*, XXXVI (May 1850), 345-346.

48

The whole representation has the dreamy yet distinct remoteness of the purely comic ideal. The view of Salem streets; the picture of the old Custom House at the head of Derby's wharf, with its torpid officers on a summer's afternoon, their chairs all tipped against the wall, chatting about old stories, "while the frozen witticisms of past generations were thawed out, and came bubbling with laughter from their lips" — the delineation of the old Inspector, whose "reminiscences of good cheer, however ancient the date of the actual banquet, seemed to bring the savor of pig or turkey under one's very nostrils," and on whose palate there were flavors "which had lingered there not less than sixty or seventy years, and were still apparently as fresh as that of the mutton-chop which he had just devoured for his breakfast," and the grand view of the stout Collector, in his aged heroism, with the honors of Chippewa and Fort Erie on his brow, are all encircled with that visionary atmosphere which proves the humorist to be a poet, and indicates that his pictures are drawn from the images which observation has left on his imagination. The whole introduction, indeed, is worthy of a place among the essays of Addison and Charles Lamb.

With regard to "The Scarlet Letter," the readers of Hawthorne might have expected an exquisitely written story, expansive in sentiment, and suggestive in characterization, but they will hardly be prepared for a novel of so much tragic interest and tragic power, so deep in thought and so condensed in style, as is here presented to them. It evinces equal genius in the region of great passions and elusive emotions, and bears on every page the evidence of a mind thoroughly alive, watching patiently the movements of morbid hearts when stirred by strange experiences, and piercing, by its imaginative power, directly through all the externals to the core of things. The fault of the book, if fault it have, is the almost morbid intensity with which the characters are realized, and the consequent lack of sufficient geniality in the delineation. A portion of the pain of the author's own heart is communicated to the reader, and although there is great pleasure received while reading the volume, the general impression left by it is not satisfying to the artistic sense. Beauty bends to power throughout the work, and therefore the power displayed is not always beautiful. There is a strange fascination to a man of contemplative genius in the psychological details of a strange crime like that which forms the plot of "The Scarlet Letter," and he is therefore apt to become, like Hawthorne, too painfully anatomical in his exhibition of them.

If there be, however, a comparative lack of relief to the painful emotions which the novel excites, owing to the intensity with which the author concentrates attention on the working of dark passions, it must be confessed that the moral purpose of the book is made more definite by this very deficiency. The most abandoned libertine could not read the volume without being thrilled into something like virtuous resolution, and the roué would find that the deep-seeing eye of the novelist had mastered the whole philosophy of that guilt of which practical roués are but childish disciples. To another class of readers, those who have theories of seduction and adultery modeled after the French school of novelists, and whom libertinism is of the brain, the volume may afford matter for very instructive and edifying contemplation; for, in truth, Hawthorne, in "The Scarlet Letter," has utterly undermined the whole philosophy on which the French novels rest, by seeing farther and deeper into the essence both of conventional and moral laws; and he has given the results of his insight, not in disquisitions and criticisms, but in representations more powerful even than those of Sue, Dumas, or George Sand. He has made his guilty parties end, not as his own fancy or his own benevolent sympathies might dictate, but as the spiritual laws, lying back of all persons, dictated to him. In this respect there is hardly a novel in English literature more purely objective.

As everybody will read "The Scarlet Letter," it would be impertinent to give a synopsis of the plot. The principal characters, Dimmesdale, Chillingworth, Hester, and little Pearl, all indicate a firm grasp of individualities, although from the peculiar method of the story, they are developed more in the way of logical analysis than by events. The descriptive portions of the novel are in a high degree picturesque and vivid, bringing the scenes directly home to the heart and imagination, and indicating a clear vision of the life as well as forms of nature. Little Pearl is perhaps Hawthorne's finest poetical creation, and is the very perfection of ideal impishness.

In common, we trust, with the rest of mankind, we regretted Hawthorne's dismissal from the Custom House, but if that event compels him to exert his genius in the production of such books as the present, we shall be inclined to class the Honorable Secretary of the Treasury among the great philanthropists. In his next work we hope to have a romance equal to "The Scarlet Letter" in pathos and power, but more relieved by touches of that beautiful and peculiar humor, so serene and so searching, in which he excels almost all living writers.

[*George Ripley*]

Review of *The Scarlet Letter*

The weird and ghostly legends of the Puritanic history present a singularly congenial field for the exercise of Mr. Hawthorne's peculiar genius. From this fruitful source he has derived the materials for his most remarkable creations. He never appears so much in his element as when threading out some dim, shadowy tradition of the twilight age of New England, peering into the faded records of our dark-visaged forefathers for the lingering traces of the preternatural, and weaving into his gorgeous web of enchantment the slender filaments which he has drawn from the distaff of some muttering witch on Gallows-Hill. He derives the same terrible excitement from these legendary horrors, as was drawn by Edgar Poe from the depths of his own dark and perilous imagination, and brings before us pictures of deathlike, but strangely fascinating agony, which are described with the same minuteness of finish — the same slow and fatal accumulation of details — the same exquisite coolness of coloring, while everything creeps forward with irresistible certainty to a soul-harrowing climax — which made the

From the New York *Daily Tribune,* April 1, 1850, p. 2; *Littell's Living Age,* xxv (May 4, 1850), 203-207.

last-named writer such a consummate master of the horrible and infernal in fictitious composition. Hawthorne's tragedies, however, are always *motived* with a wonderful insight and skill, to which the intellect of Poe was a stranger. In the most terrific scenes with which he delights to scare the imagination, Hawthorne does not wander into the region of the improbable; you scarcely know that you are in the presence of the supernatural, until your breathing becomes too thick for this world; it is the supernatural relieved, softened, made tolerable, and almost attractive, by a strong admixture of the human; you are tempted onward by the mild, unearthly light, which seems to shine upon you like a healthful star; you are blinded by no lurid glare; you acquiesce in the necessity of the wizard journey; instead of being provoked to anger by a superfluous introduction to the company of the devil and his angels.

The elements of terror, which Mr. Hawthorne employs with such masterly effect, both in the original conception of his characters and the scenes of mystery and dread in which they are made to act, are blended with such sweet gushes of natural feeling, such solemn and tender relations of the deepest secrets of the heart, that the painful impression is greatly mitigated, and the final influence of his most startling creation is a serene sense of refreshment, without the stupor and bewilderment occasioned by a drugged cup of intoxication.

The "Scarlet Letter," in our opinion, is the greatest production of the author, beautifully displaying the traits we have briefly hinted at, and sustained with a more vigorous reach of imagination, a more subtle instinct of humanity, and a more imposing splendor of portraiture, than any of his most successful previous works. . . .

This mysterious being, who holds a principal place in the development of the plot, is depicted with such fearful distinctness and vigor that his infernal presence must long haunt the chambers of memory.

A creation of a different order, but of no less originality and power, gleams in fairy brightness through the sombre scenes of the narrative, surpassing in artistic harmony, and in mystic, thrilling grace, the similar productions of Goethe and Scott. . . .

The grouping in this drama of indescribable misery is completed by the person of the Reverend Arthur Dimmesdale, of whose character we are put fully in possession by a description black with harrowing agony. . . .

We have not intended to forestall our readers with a description of the plot, which it will be perceived abounds in elements of tragic

interest, but to present them with some specimens of a genuine
native romance, which none will be content without reading for
themselves. The moral of the story — for it has a moral for all
wise enough to detect it — is shadowed forth rather than expressed
in a few brief sentences near the close of the volume. . . .

The introduction, presenting a record of savory reminiscences of
the Salem Custom House, a frank display of autobiographical
confessions, and a piquant daguerreotype of his ancient colleagues
in office, while surveyor of that port, is written with Mr. Hawthorne's
unrivalled force of graphic delineation, and will furnish an agreeable
amusement to those who are so far from the scene of action as to
feel no wound in their personal relations, by the occasional too
sharp touches of the caustic acid, of which the "gentle author"
keeps some phials on his shelf for convenience and use. The
querulous tone in which he alludes to his removal from the Custom
House, may be forgiven to the sensitiveness of a poet, especially as
this is so rare a quality in Uncle Sam's office-holders.

[Henry F. Chorley]

Review of *The Scarlet Letter*

This is a most powerful but painful story. Mr. Hawthorne must
be well known to our readers as a favourite with the *Athenaeum*.
We rate him as among the most original and peculiar writers of
American fiction. There is in his works a mixture of Puritan reserve
and wild imagination, of passion and description, of the allegorical
and the real, which some will fail to understand, and which others
will positively reject, — but which, to ourselves, is fascinating, and
which entitles him to be placed on a level with Brockden Brown
and the author of "Rip Van Winkle." "The Scarlet Letter" will
increase his reputation with all who do not shrink from the inven-
tion of the tale; but this, as we have said, is more than ordinarily
painful. When we have announced that the three characters are a
guilty wife, openly punished for her guilt, — her tempter, whom
she refuses to unmask, and who during the entire story carries a
fair front and an unblemished name among his congregation, — and
her husband, who, returning from a long absence at the moment
of her sentence, sits himself down betwixt the two in the midst

From the London *Athenaeum,* No. 1181 (June 15, 1850), p. 634.

of a small and severe community to work out his slow vengeance on both under the pretext of magnanimous forgiveness, — when we have explained that "The Scarlet Letter" is the badge of Hester Prynne's shame, we ought to add that we recollect no tale dealing with crime so sad and revenge so subtly diabolical, that is at the same time so clear of fever and of prurient excitement. The misery of the woman is as present in every page as the heading which in the title of the romance symbolizes her punishment. Her terrors concerning her strange elvish child present retribution in a form which is new and natural: — her slow and painful purification through repentance is crowned by no perfect happiness, such as awaits the decline of those who have no dark and bitter past to remember. Then, the gradual corrosion of heart of Dimmesdale, the faithless priest, under the insidious care of the husband, (whose relationship to Hester is a secret known only to themselves,) is appalling; and his final confession and expiation are merely a relief, not a reconciliation. — We are by no means satisfied that passions and tragedies like these are the legitimate subjects for fiction; we are satisfied that novels such as "Adam Blair" and plays such as "The Stranger" may be justly charged with attracting more persons than they warn by their excitement. But if Sin and Sorrow in their most fearful forms are to be presented in any work of art, they have rarely been treated with a loftier severity, purity, and sympathy than in Mr. Hawthorne's "Scarlet Letter." The touch of the fantastic befitting a period of society in which ignorant and excitable human creatures conceived each other and themselves to be under the direct "rule and governance" of the Wicked One, is most skilfully administered. The supernatural here never becomes grossly palpable: — the thrill is all the deeper for its action being indefinite, and its source vague and distant.

3. In the Era of the Realistic Novel

Henry James

From "The Three American Novels"

The prospect of official station and emolument which Hawthorne mentions in one of those paragraphs from his Journals which I have just quoted, as having offered itself and then passed away, was at last, in the event, confirmed by his receiving from the administration of President Polk the gift of a place in the Custom-house of his native town. The office was a modest one, and "official station" may perhaps appear a magniloquent formula for the functions sketched in the admirable Introduction to *The Scarlet Letter*. Hawthorne's duties were those of Surveyor of the port of Salem, and they had a salary attached, which was the important part; as his biographer tells us that he had received almost nothing for the contributions to the *Democratic Review*. He bade farewell to his ex-parsonage, and went back to Salem in 1846, and the immediate effect of his ameliorated fortune was to make him stop writing. None of his Journals of the period, from his going to Salem to 1850, have been published; from which I infer that he even ceased to journalise. *The Scarlet Letter* was not written till

From *Hawthorne* (New York, 1879), pp. 102-117.

1849. In the delightful prologue to that work, entitled *The Custom=house*, he embodies some of the impressions gathered during these years of comparative leisure (I say of leisure, because he does not intimate in this sketch of his occupations that his duties were onerous). He intimates, however, that they were not interesting, and that it was a very good thing for him, mentally and morally, when his term of service expired — or rather when he was removed from office by the operation of that wonderful "rotatory" system which his countrymen had invented for the administration of their affairs. This sketch of the Custom-house is, as simple writing, one of the most perfect of Hawthorne's compositions, and one of the most gracefully and humorously autobiographic. It would be interesting to examine it in detail, but I prefer to use my space for making some remarks upon the work which was the ultimate result of this period of Hawthorne's residence in his native town; and I shall, for convenience' sake, say directly afterwards what I have to say about the two companions of *The Scarlet Letter* — *The House of the Seven Gables* and *The Blithedale Romance*. I quoted some passages from the prologue to the first of these novels in the early pages of this essay. There is another passage, however, which bears particularly upon this phase of Hawthorne's career, and which is so happily expressed as to make it a pleasure to transcribe it — the passage in which he says that "for myself, during the whole of my Custom-house experience, moonlight and sunshine, and the glow of the firelight, were just alike in my regard, and neither of them was of one whit more avail than the twinkle of a tallow-candle. An entire class of susceptibilities, and a gift connected with them — of no great richness or value, but the best I had — was gone from me." He goes on to say that he believes that he might have done something if he could have made up his mind to convert the very substance of the commonplace that surrounded him into matter of literature.

> I might, for instance, have contented myself with writing out the narratives of a veteran shipmaster, one of the inspectors, whom I should be most ungrateful not to mention; since scarcely a day passed that he did not stir me to laughter and admiration by his marvellous gift as a story-teller. . . . Or I might readily have found a more serious task. It was a folly, with the materiality of this daily life pressing so intrusively upon me, to attempt to fling myself back into another age; or to insist on creating a semblance of a world out of airy matter. . . . The wiser effort would have been, to diffuse

thought and imagination through the opaque substance of to-day, and thus make it a bright transparency . . . to seek resolutely the true and indestructible value that lay hidden in the petty and wearisome incidents and ordinary characters with which I was now conversant. The fault was mine. The page of life that was spread out before me was dull and commonplace, only because I had not fathomed its deeper import. A better book than I shall ever write was there. . . . These perceptions came too late. . . . I had ceased to be a writer of tolerably poor tales and essays, and had become a tolerably good Surveyor of the Customs. That was all. But, nevertheless, it is anything but agreeable to be haunted by a suspicion that one's intellect is dwindling away, or exhaling, without your consciousness, like ether out of phial; so that at every glance you find a smaller and less volatile residuum.

As, however, it was with what was left of his intellect after three years' evaporation, that Hawthorne wrote *The Scarlet Letter,* there is little reason to complain of the injury he suffered in his Surveyorship.

His publisher, Mr. Fields, in a volume entitled *Yesterdays with Authors,* has related the circumstances in which Hawthorne's masterpiece came into the world. "In the winter of 1849, after he had been ejected from the Custom-house, I went down to Salem to see him and inquire after his health, for we heard he had been suffering from illness. He was then living in a modest wooden house. . . . I found him alone in a chamber over the sitting-room of the dwelling, and as the day was cold he was hovering near a stove. We fell into talk about his future prospects, and he was, as I feared I should find him, in a very desponding mood." His visitor urged him to bethink himself of publishing something, and Hawthorne replied by calling his attention to the small popularity his published productions had yet acquired, and declaring he had done nothing, and had no spirit for doing anything. The narrator of the incident urged upon him the necessity of a more hopeful view of his situation, and proceeded to take leave. He had not reached the street, however, when Hawthorne hurried to overtake him, and, placing a roll of MS. in his hand, bade him take it to Boston, read it, and pronounce upon it. "It is either very good or very bad," said the author; "I don't know which." "On my way back to Boston," says Mr. Fields, "I read the germ of *The Scarlet Letter;* before I slept that night I wrote him a note all aglow with admiration of the marvellous story he had put into my hands, and told him that I would come again to Salem the next day and arrange for its publication. I went on in such an amazing state of excitement, when we met again in the little house, that he would not believe I was really in earnest. He seemed to think I was beside myself, and laughed sadly at my enthusiasm." Hawthorne, however, went on with the book and finished it, but it appeared only a year later. His biographer quotes a passage from a letter which he wrote in February, 1850, to his friend Horatio Bridge. "I finished my book only yesterday; one end being in the press at Boston, while the other was in my head here at Salem; so that, as you see, my story is at least fourteen miles long. . . . My book, the publisher tells me, will not be out before April. He speaks of it in tremendous terms of approbation; so does Mrs. Hawthorne, to whom I read the conclusion last night. It broke her heart, and sent her to bed with a grievous headache — which I look upon as a triumphant success. Judging from the effect upon her and the publisher, I may calculate on what bowlers call a ten-strike. But I don't make any such calculation." And Mr. Lathrop calls attention, in regard to this passage, to an allusion in the English Note-Books (September 14, 1855). "Speaking of Thackeray, I cannot but wonder at his coolness in respect to his own pathos, and compare it to my own emotions when I read the last scene of *The Scarlet Letter* to my wife, just after writing it — tried to read it, rather, for my voice swelled and heaved as if I were tossed up and down on an ocean as it subsides after a storm. But I was in a very nervous state then, having gone through a great diversity of emotion while writing it, for many months."

The work has the tone of the circumstances in which it was produced. If Hawthorne was in a sombre mood, and if his future was painfully vague, *The Scarlet Letter* contains little enough of gaiety or of hopefulness. It is densely dark, with a single spot of vivid colour in it; and it will probably long remain the most consistently gloomy of English novels of the first order. But I just now called it the author's masterpiece, and I imagine it will continue to be, for other generations than ours, his most substantial title to fame. The subject had probably lain a long time in his mind, as his subjects were apt to do; so that he appears completely to possess it, to know it and feel it. It is simpler and more complete than his other novels; it achieves more perfectly what it attempts, and it has about it that charm, very hard to express, which we find in an artist's work the first time he has touched his highest mark — a sort of straightness and naturalness of execution, an unconsciousness of his public, and freshness of interest in his theme.

It was a great success, and he immediately found himself famous. The writer of these lines, who was a child at the time, remembers dimly the sensation the book produced, and the little shudder with which people alluded to it, as if a peculiar horror were mixed with its attractions. He was too young to read it himself; but its title, upon which he fixed his eyes as the book lay upon the table, had a mysterious charm. He had a vague belief, indeed, that the "letter" in question was one of the documents that come by the post, and it was a source of perpetual wonderment to him that it should be of such an unaccustomed hue. Of course it was difficult to explain to a child the significance of poor Hester Prynne's blood-coloured *A*. But the mystery was at last partly dispelled by his being taken to see a collection of pictures (the annual exhibition of the National Academy), where he encountered a representation of a pale, handsome woman, in a quaint black dress and a white coif, holding between her knees an elfish-looking little girl, fantastically dressed, and crowned with flowers. Embroidered on the woman's breast was a great crimson *A*, over which the child's fingers, as she glanced strangely out of the picture, were maliciously playing. I was told that this was Hester Prynne and little Pearl, and that when I grew older I might read their interesting history. But the picture remained vividly imprinted on my mind; I had been vaguely frightened and made uneasy by it; and when, years afterwards, I first read the novel, I seemed to myself to have read it before, and to be familiar with its two strange heroines. I mention this incident simply as an indication of the degree to which the success of *The Scarlet Letter* had made the book what is called an actuality. Hawthorne himself was very modest about it; he wrote to his publisher, when there was a question of his undertaking another novel, that what had given the history of Hester Prynne its "vogue" was simply the introductory chapter. In fact, the publication of *The Scarlet Letter* was in the United States a literary event of the first importance. The book was the finest piece of imaginative writing yet put forth in the country. There was a consciousness of this in the welcome that was given it — a satisfaction in the idea of America having produced a novel that belonged to literature, and to the forefront of it. Something might at last be sent to Europe as exquisite in quality as anything that had been received, and the best of it was that the thing was absolutely American; it belonged to the soil, to the air; it came out of the very heart of New England.

It is beautiful, admirable, extraordinary; it has in the highest degree that merit which I have spoken of as the mark of Hawthorne's best things — an indefinable purity and lightness of conception, a quality which in a work of art affects one in the same way as the absence of grossness does in a human being. His fancy, as I just now said, had evidently brooded over the subject for a long time; the situation to be represented had disclosed itself to him in all its phases. When I say in all its phases, the sentence demands modification; for it is to be remembered that if Hawthorne laid his hand upon the well-worn theme, upon the familiar combination of the wife, the lover, and the husband, it was, after all, but to one period of the history of these three persons that he attached himself. The situation is the situation after the woman's fault has been committed, and the current of expiation and repentance has set in. In spite of the relation between Hester Prynne and Arthur Dimmesdale, no story of love was surely ever less of a "love-story." To Hawthorne's imagination the fact that these two persons had loved each other too well was of an interest comparatively vulgar; what appealed to him was the idea of their moral situation in the long years that were to follow. The story, indeed, is in a secondary degree that of Hester Prynne; she becomes, really, after the first scene, an accessory figure; it is not upon her the *dénoûment* depends. It is upon her guilty lover that the author projects most frequently the cold, thin rays of his fitfully-moving lantern, which makes here and there a little luminous circle, on the edge of which hovers the livid and sinister figure of the injured and retributive husband. The story goes on, for the most part, between the lover and the husband — the tormented young Puritan minister, who carries the secret of his own lapse from pastoral purity locked up beneath an exterior that commends itself to the reverence of his flock, while he sees the softer partner of his guilt standing in the full glare of exposure and humbling herself to the misery of atonement — between this more wretched and pitiable culprit, to whom dishonour would come as a comfort and the pillory as a relief, and the older, keener, wiser man, who, to obtain satisfaction for the wrong he has suffered, devises the infernally ingenious plan of conjoining himself with his wronger, living with him, living upon him; and while he pretends to minister to his hidden ailment and to sympathise with his pain, revels in his unsuspected knowledge of these things, and stimulates them by malignant arts. The attitude of Roger Chillingworth, and the means he takes to compensate himself — these are the highly original elements in the situation that Hawthorne so ingeniously treats. None of his works are so impregnated with that after-sense of the old Puritan consciousness of life to which allusion has so often been made. If, as M. Montégut says, the qualities of his ancestors *filtered* down through generations into his composition, *The Scarlet Letter* was, as it were, the vessel that gathered up the last of the precious drops. And I say this not because the story happens to be of so-called historical cast, to be told of the early days of Massachusetts, and of people in steeple-crowned hats and sad-coloured garments. The historical colouring is rather weak than otherwise; there is little elaboration of detail, of the modern realism of research; and the author has made no great point of causing his figures to speak the English of their period. Nevertheless, the book is full of the moral presence of the race that invented Hester's penance — diluted and complicated with other things, but still perfectly recognisable. Puritanism, in a word, is there, not only objectively, as Hawthorne tried to place it there, but subjectively as well. Not, I mean, in his judgment of his characters in any harshness of prejudice, or in the obtrusion of a moral lesson; but in the very quality of his own vision, in the tone of the picture, in a certain coldness and exclusiveness of treatment.

The faults of the book are, to my sense, a want of reality and an abuse of the fanciful element — of a certain superficial symbolism. The people strike me not as characters, but as representatives, very picturesquely arranged, of a single state of mind; and the interest of the story lies, not in them, but in the situation, which is insistently kept before us, with little progression, though with a great deal, as I have said, of a certain stable variation; and to which they, out of their reality, contribute little that helps it to live and move. I was made to feel this want of reality, this over-ingenuity, of *The Scarlet Letter*, by chancing not long since upon a novel which was read fifty years ago much more than to-day, but which is still worth reading — the story of *Adam Blair*, by John Gibson Lockhart. This interesting and powerful little tale has a great deal of analogy with Hawthorne's novel — quite enough, at least, to suggest a comparison between them; and the comparison is a very interesting one to make, for it speedily leads us to larger considerations than simple resemblances and divergences of plot.

Adam Blair, like Arthur Dimmesdale, is a Calvinistic minister who becomes the lover of a married woman, is overwhelmed with remorse at his misdeed, and makes a public confession of it; then expiates it by resigning his pastoral office and becoming a humble tiller of the soil, as his father had been. The two stories are of about the same length, and each is the masterpiece (putting aside, of course, as far as Lockhart is concerned, the *Life of Scott*) of the author. They deal alike with the manners of a rigidly theological society, and even in certain details they correspond. In each of them, between the guilty pair, there is a charming little girl; though I hasten to say that Sarah Blair (who is not the daughter of the heroine, but the legitimate offspring of the hero, a widower) is far from being as brilliant and graceful an apparition as the admirable little Pearl of *The Scarlet Letter*. The main difference between the two tales is the fact that in the American story the husband plays an all-important part, and in the Scottish plays almost none at all. *Adam Blair* is the history of the passion, and *The Scarlet Letter* the history of its sequel; but nevertheless, if one has read the two books at a short interval, it is impossible to avoid confronting them. I confess that a large portion of the interest of *Adam Blair*, to my mind, when once I had perceived that it would repeat in a great measure the situation of *The Scarlet Letter*, lay in noting its difference of tone. It threw into relief the passionless quality of Hawthorne's novel, its element of cold and ingenious fantasy, its elaborate imaginative delicacy. These things do not precisely constitute a weakness in *The Scarlet Letter;* indeed, in a certain way they constitute a great strength; but the absence of a certain something warm and straightforward, a trifle more grossly human and vulgarly natural, which one finds in *Adam Blair*, will always make Hawthorne's tale less touching to a large number of even very intelligent readers, than a love-story told with the robust, synthetic pathos which served Lockhart so well. His novel is not of the first rank (I should call it an excellent second-rate one), but it borrows a charm from the fact that his vigorous, but not strongly imaginative, mind was impregnated with the reality of his subject. He did not always succeed in rendering this reality; the expression is sometimes awkward and poor. But the reader feels that his vision was clear, and his feeling about the matter very strong and rich. Hawthorne's imagination, on the other hand, plays with his theme so incessantly, leads it such a dance through the moon-lighted air of his intellect, that the thing cools off, as it were, hardens and stiffens, and, producing effects much more exquisite, leaves the reader with a sense of having handled a splendid piece of silversmith's work. Lockhart, by means much more vulgar, produces at moments a greater illusion, and satisfies our inevitable desire for something, in the people in whom it is sought to interest us, that shall be of the same pitch and the same continuity with ourselves. Above all, it is interesting to see how the same subject appears to two men of a thoroughly different cast of mind and of a different race. Lockhart was struck with the warmth of the subject that offered itself to him, and Hawthorne with its coldness; the one with its glow, its sentimental interest — the other with its shadow, its moral interest. Lockhart's story is as decent, as severely draped, as *The Scarlet Letter;* but the author has a more vivid sense than appears to have imposed itself upon Hawthorne, of some of the incidents of the situation he describes; his tempted man and tempting woman are more actual and personal; his heroine in especial, though not in the least a delicate or a subtle conception, has a sort of credible, visible, palpable property, a vulgar roundness and relief, which are lacking to the dim and chastened image of Hester Prynne. But I am going too far; I am comparing simplicity with subtlety, the usual with the refined. Each man wrote as his turn of mind impelled him, but each expressed something more than himself. Lockhart was a dense, substantial Briton, with a taste for the concrete, and Hawthorne was a thin New Englander, with a miasmatic conscience.

In *The Scarlet Letter* there is a great deal of symbolism; there is, I think, too much. It is overdone at times, and becomes mechanical; it ceases to be impressive, and grazes triviality. The idea of the mystic *A* which the young minister finds imprinted upon his breast and eating into his flesh, in sympathy with the embroidered badge that Hester is condemned to wear, appears to me to be a case in point. This suggestion should, I think, have been just made and dropped; to insist upon it and return to it, is to exaggerate the weak side of the subject. Hawthorne returns to it constantly, plays with it, and seems charmed by it; until at last the reader feels tempted to declare that his enjoyment of it is puerile. In the admirable scene, so superbly conceived and beautifully executed, in which Mr. Dimmesdale, in the stillness of the night, in the middle of the sleeping town, feels impelled to go and stand upon the scaffold where his mistress had formerly enacted her dreadful penance, and then, seeing Hester pass along the street, from watching at a sick-bed, with little Pearl at her side, calls them both to come and stand there beside him — in this masterly episode the effect is almost spoiled by the introduction of one of these superficial conceits. What leads up to it is very fine — so fine that I cannot do better than quote it as a specimen of one of the striking pages of the book.

But before Mr. Dimmesdale had done speaking, a light gleamed far and wide over all the muffled sky. It was doubtless caused by one of those meteors which the night-watcher may so often observe burning out to waste in the vacant regions of the atmosphere. So powerful was its radiance that it thoroughly illuminated the dense medium of cloud betwixt the sky and earth. The great vault brightened, like the dome of an immense lamp. It showed the familiar scene of the street with the distinctness of mid-day, but also with the awfulness that is always imparted to familiar objects by an unaccustomed light. The wooden houses, with their jutting stories and quaint gable-peaks; the doorsteps and thresholds, with the early grass springing up about them; the garden-plots, black with freshly-turned earth; the wheel-track, little worn, and, even in the market-place, margined with green on either side;—all were visible, but with a singularity of aspect that seemed to give another moral interpretation to the things of this world than they had ever borne before. And there stood the minister, with his hand over his heart; and Hester Prynne, with the embroidered letter glimmering on her bosom; and little Pearl, herself a symbol, and the connecting link between these two. They stood in the noon of that strange and solemn splendour, as if it were the light that is to reveal all secrets, and the daybreak that shall unite all that belong to one another.

That is imaginative, impressive, poetic; but when, almost immediately afterwards, the author goes on to say that "the minister looking upward to the zenith, beheld there the appearance of an immense letter — the letter *A* — marked out in lines of dull red light," we feel that he goes too far, and is in danger of crossing the line that separates the sublime from its intimate neighbour. We are tempted to say that this is not moral tragedy, but physical comedy. In the same way, too much is made of the intimation that Hester's badge had a scorching property, and that if one touched it one would immediately withdraw one's hand. Hawthorne is perpetually looking for images which shall place themselves in picturesque correspondence with the spiritual facts with which he is concerned, and of course the search is of the very essence of poetry. But in such a process discretion is everything, and when the image becomes importunate it is in danger of seeming to stand for nothing more serious than itself. When Hester meets the minister by appointment in the forest, and sits talking with him while little Pearl wanders away and plays by the edge of the brook, the child is represented as at last making her way over to the other side of the woodland stream, and disporting herself there in a manner which makes her mother feel herself, "in some indistinct and tantalising manner, estranged from Pearl; as if the child, in her lonely ramble through the forest, had strayed out of the sphere in which she and her mother dwelt together, and was now vainly seeking to return to it." And Hawthorne devotes a chapter to this idea of the child's having, by putting the brook between Hester and herself, established a kind of spiritual gulf, on the verge of which her little fantastic person innocently mocks at her mother's sense of bereavement. This conception belongs, one would say, quite to the lighter order of a story-teller's devices, and the reader hardly goes with Hawthorne in the large development he gives to it. He hardly goes with him either, I think, in his extreme predilection for a small number of vague ideas which are represented by such terms as "sphere" and "sympathies." Hawthorne makes too liberal a use of these two substantives; it is the solitary defect of his style; and it counts as a defect partly because the words in question are a sort of specialty with certain writers immeasurably inferior to himself.

I had not meant, however, to expatiate upon his defects, which are of the slenderest and most venial kind. *The Scarlet Letter* has the beauty and harmony of all original and complete conceptions, and its weaker spots, whatever they are, are not of its essence; they are mere light flaws and inequalities of surface. One can often return to it; it supports familiarity, and has the inexhaustible charm and mystery of great works of art. It is admirably written. Hawthorne afterwards polished his style to a still higher degree; but in his later productions — it is almost always the case in a writer's later productions — there is a touch of mannerism. In *The Scarlet Letter* there is a high degree of polish, and at the same time a charming freshness; his phrase is less conscious of itself. His biographer very justly calls attention to the fact that his style was excellent from the beginning; that he appeared to have passed through no phase of learning how to write, but was in possession of his means, from the first, of his handling a pen. His early tales, perhaps, were not of a character to subject his faculty of expression to a very severe test; but a man who had not Hawthorne's natural sense of language would certainly have contrived to write them less well. This natural sense of language — this turn for saying things lightly and yet touchingly, picturesquely yet simply, and for infusing a gently colloquial tone into matter of the most unfamiliar import — he had evidently cultivated with great assiduity. I have spoken of the anomalous character of his Note-Books — of his going to such pains often to make a record of incidents which either were not worth remembering, or could be easily remembered without its aid. But it helps us to understand the Note-Books if we regard them as a literary exercise. They were compositions, as schoolboys say, in which the subject was only the pretext, and the main point was to write a certain amount of excellent English. Hawthorne must at least have written a great many of these things for practice, and he must often have said to himself that it was better practice to write about trifles, because it was a greater tax upon one's skill to make them interesting. And his theory was just, for he has almost always made his trifles interesting. In his novels his art of saying things well is very positively tested; for here he treats of those matters among which it is very easy for a blundering writer to go wrong — the subtleties and mysteries of life, the moral and spiritual maze. In such a passage as one I have marked for quotation from *The Scarlet Letter*, there is the stamp of the genius of style. . . .

Anthony Trollope

From "The Genius of
Nathaniel Hawthorne"

There never surely was a powerful, active, continually effective mind less round, more lop-sided, than that of Nathaniel Hawthorne. If there were aught of dispraise in this, it would not be said by me, — by an Englishman of an American whom I knew, by an Englishman of letters of a brother on the other side of the water, much less by me, an English novelist, of an American novelist. The blacksmith, who is abnormally strong in his arm, gives the world the advantage of his strength. The poor bird, whose wretched life is sacrified to the unnatural growth of that portion of him which the gourmands love, does produce the desired dainties in all their perfection. We could have hardly had "Childe Harold" except from a soured nature. The seraphic excellence of "Hiawatha" and "Evangeline" could have proceeded only from a mind which the world's roughness had neither toughened nor tainted. So from Hawthorne we could not have obtained that weird, mysterious, thrilling charm with which he has awed and delighted us had he

From "The Genius of Nathaniel Hawthorne," *North American Review,* CXXIX (September 1879), 204-213.

not allowed his mind to revel in one direction, so as to lose its fair proportions.

I have been specially driven to think of this by the strong divergence between Hawthorne and myself. It has always been my object to draw my little pictures as like to life as possible, so that my readers should feel that they were dealing with people whom they might probably have known, but so to do it that the every-day good to be found among them should allure, and the every-day evil repel; and this I have attempted, believing that such ordinary good and ordinary evil would be more powerful in repelling or alluring than great and glowing incidents which, though they might interest, would not come home to the minds of readers. Hawthorne, on the other hand, has dealt with persons and incidents which were often but barely within the bounds of possibility, — which were sometimes altogether without those bounds, — and has determined that his readers should be carried out of their own little mundane ways, and brought into a world of imagination in which their intelligence might be raised, if only for a time, to something higher than the common needs of common life.

I will venture here to quote an extract from a letter written by Hawthorne to an American gentleman, a friend of his, — and of mine, though, if I remember rightly, I did not get it from him, — which he will recognize should he see this paper. As it is altogether about myself, perhaps I should do better to keep it to myself, but I will give it because it explains so accurately his own condition of mind in regard to novels; "It is odd enough that my own individual taste is for quite another class of novels than those which I myself am able to write. If I were to meet with such books as mine by another writer, I don't believe I should be able to get through them. Have you ever read the novels of Anthony Trollope? They precisely suit my taste; solid and substantial, written on strength of beef and through the inspiration of ale, and just as real as if some giant had hewn a great lump out of the earth, and put it under a glass case, with all its inhabitants going about their daily business, and not suspecting that they were made a show of." This is what he could read himself, but could not possibly have produced, — any more than I could have produced that "Marble Faun" which has been quite as much to my taste as was to his the fragment of common life which he has supposed me to put under a glass case in order that the frequenters at my little show might inspect at their ease all that was being done on that morsel of the earth's surface. How was it that his mind wandered away always into those fancies, not jocund as are usually those of the tellers of fairly tales, not high-flown as are the pictures generally drawn by the poets, with no fearful adventures though so sad, often by no means beautiful, without an attempt even at the picturesque, melancholy beyond compare, as though the writer had drawn all his experiences from untoward accidents? That some remnant of Puritan asceticism should be found in the writings of a novelist from Concord, in Massachusetts, would seem natural to an English reader, — though I doubt whether there be much of the flavor of the Mayflower left at present to pervade the literary parterres of Boston. But, had that been the Hawthorne flavor, readers both in England and in the States would have accepted it without surprise.

It is, however, altogether different, though ascetic enough. The predominating quality of Puritan life was hard, good sense,—a good sense which could value the realities of life while it rejected the frivolities, — a good sense to which buttered cakes, water-tight boots, and a pretty wife, or a kind husband could endear themselves. Hawthorne is severe, but his severity is never of a nature to form laws for life. His is a mixture of romance and austerity, quite as far removed from the realities of Puritanism as it is from the sentimentalism of poetry. He creates a melancholy which amounts almost to remorse in the minds of his readers. There falls upon them a conviction of some unutterable woe which is not altogether dispelled till other books and other incidents have had their effects. The woe is of course fictitious, and therefore endurable, — and therefore alluring. And woe itself has its charm. It is a fact that the really miserable will pity the comfortable insignificance of those who are not unhappy, and that they are apt even to boast of their own sufferings. There is a sublimity in mental and even in corporal torment which will sometimes make the position of Lucifer almost enviable. "All is not lost" with him! Prometheus chained, with the bird at his liver, had wherewithal to console himself in the magnificence of his thoughts. And so in the world of melancholy romance, of agony more realistic than melancholy, to which Hawthorne brings his readers, there is compensation to the reader in the feeling that, in having submitted himself to such sublime affliction, he has proved himself capable of sublimity. The bird that feeds upon your vitals would not have gorged himself with common flesh. You are beyond measure depressed by the weird tale that is told to you, but you become conscious of a certain grandness of nature in being susceptible of such suffering. When you hear what Hawthorne has done to others, you long to search his volumes. When he has operated upon you, you would not for worlds have foregone it. You have been ennobled by that familiarity with sorrow. You have been, as it were, sent through the fire and purged of so much of your dross. For a time, at least, you have been free from the mundane touch of that beef and ale with which novelists of a meaner school will certainly bring you in contact. No one will feel himself ennobled at once by having read one of my novels. But Hawthorne, when you have studied him, will be very precious to you. He will have plunged you into melancholy, he will have overshadowed you with black forebodings, he will almost have crushed you with imaginary sorrows; but he will have enabled you to feel yourself an inch taller during the process. Something of the sublimity of the transcendent, something of the mystery of the unfathomable, something of the brightness of the celestial, will have attached itself to you, and you will all but think that you too might live to be sublime, and revel in mingled light and mystery.

The creations of American literature generally are no doubt more given to the speculative, — less given to the realistic, — than are those of English literature. On our side of the water we deal more with beef and ale, and less with dreams. Even with the broad humor of Bret Harte, even with the broader humor of Artemus Ward and Mark Twain, there is generally present an undercurrent of melancholy, in which pathos and satire are intermingled. There was a touch of it even with the simple-going Cooper and the kindly Washington Irving. Melancholy and pathos, without the humor, are the springs on which all Longfellow's lines are set moving. But in no American writer is to be found the same predominance of weird imagination as in Hawthorne. There was something of it in M. G. Lewis — our Monk Lewis as he came to be called, from the name of a tale which he wrote; but with him, as with many others, we feel that they have been weird because they have desired to be so. They have struggled to achieve the tone with which their works are pervaded. With Hawthorne we are made to think that he could not have been anything else if he would. It is as though he could certainly have been nothing else in his own inner life. We know that such was not actually the case. Though a man singularly reticent, — what we generally call shy, — he could, when things went well with him, be argumentative, social, and cheery. I have seen him very happy over canvas-back ducks, and have heard him discuss, almost with violence, the superiority of American vegetables. Indeed, he once withered me with a scorn which was anything but mystic or melancholy because I expressed a patriotic preference for English peas. And yet his imagination was such that the creations of his brain could not have been other than such as I have described. Oliver Wendell Holmes has written a well-known story, weird and witch-like also, and has displayed much genius in the picture which he has given us of Elsie Venner. But the reader is at once aware that Holmes compelled himself to the construction of "Elsie Venner," and feels equally sure that Hawthorne wrote "The Marble Faun" because he could not help himself.

I will take a few of his novels, — those which I believe to be the best known, — and will endeavor to illustrate my idea of his genius by describing the manner in which his stories have been told.

"The Scarlet Letter" is, on the English side of the water, perhaps the best known. It is so terrible in its pictures of diseased human nature as to produce most questionable delight. The reader's interest never flags for a moment. There is nothing of episode or digression. The author is always telling his one story with a concentration of energy which, as we can understand, must have made it impossible for him to deviate. The reader will certainly go on with it to the end very quickly, entranced, excited, shuddering, and at times almost wretched. His consolation will be that he too has been able to see into these black deeps of the human heart. The story is one of jealousy, — of love and jealousy, — in which love is allowed but little scope, but full play is given to the hatred which can spring from injured love. A woman has been taken in adultery, — among the Puritans of Boston some two centuries since, — and is brought upon the stage that she may be punished by a public stigma. She was beautiful and young, and had been married to an old husband who had wandered away from her for a time. Then she has sinned, and the partner of her sin, though not of her punishment, is the young minister of the church to which she is attached. It is her doom to wear the Scarlet Letter, the letter A, always worked on her dress, — always there on her bosom, to be seen by all men. The first hour of her punishment has to be endured, in the middle of the town, on the public scaffold, under the gaze of all men. As she stands there, her husband comes by chance into the town and sees her, and she sees him, and they know each other. But no one else in Boston knows that they are man and wife. Then they meet, and she refuses to tell him who has been her fellow sinner. She makes no excuse for herself. She will bear her doom and acknowledge its justice, but to no one will she

tell the name of him who is the father of her baby. For her disgrace
has borne its fruit, and she has a child. The injured husband is at
once aware that he need deal no further with the woman who has
been false to him. Her punishment is sure. But it is necessary for
his revenge that the man too shall be punished, — and to punish
him he must know him. He goes to work to find him out, and he
finds him out. Then he does punish him with a vengeance and brings
him to death, — does it by the very stress of mental misery. After
a while the woman turns and rebels against the atrocity of fate, —
not on her own account, but for the sake of that man the sight
of whose sufferings she can not bear. They meet once again, the
two sinful lovers, and a hope of escape comes upon them, — and
another gleam of love. But fate in the shape of the old man is
too strong for them. He finds them out, and, not stopping to hinder
their flight, merely declares his purpose of accompanying them!
Then the lover succumbs and dies, and the woman is left to her
solitude. That is the story.

The personages in it with whom the reader will interest himself
are four, — the husband, the minister who has been the sinful lover,
the woman, and the child. The reader is expected to sympathize
only with the woman, — and will sympathize only with her. The
husband, an old man who has knowingly married a young woman
who did not love him, is a personification of that feeling of injury
which is supposed to fall upon a man when his honor has been
stained by the falseness of a wife. He has left her and has wandered
away, not even telling her of his whereabout. He comes back to
her without a sign. The author tells us that he had looked to find
his happiness in her solicitude and care for him. The reader, however, gives him credit for no love. But the woman was his wife,
and he comes back and finds that she had gone astray. Her he
despises, and is content to leave to the ascetic cruelty of the town
magistrates; but to find the man out and bring the man to his
grave by slow torture is enough of employment for what is left to
him of life and energy.

With the man, the minister, the lover, the reader finds that he
can have nothing in common, though he is compelled to pity his
sufferings. The woman has held her peace when she was discovered
and reviled and exposed. She will never whisper his name, never
call on him for any comfort or support in her misery; but he,
though the very shame is eating into his soul, lives through the
seven years of the story, a witness of her misery and solitude, while
he himself is surrounded by the very glory of sanctity. Of the two,

indeed, he is the greater sufferer. While shame only deals with her, conscience is at work with him. But there can be no sympathy, because he looks on and holds his peace. Her child says to him, — her child, not knowing that he is her father, not knowing what she says, but in answer to him when he would fain take her little hand in his during the darkness of night, — "Wilt thou stand here with mother and me to-morrow noontide"? He can not bring himself to do that, though he struggles hard to do it, and therefore we despise him. He can not do it till the hand of death is upon him, and then the time is too late for reparation in the reader's judgment. Could we have sympathized with a pair of lovers, the human element would have prevailed too strongly for the author's purpose.

He seems hardly to have wished that we should sympathize even with her; or, at any rate, he has not bid us in so many words to do so, as is common with authors. Of course, he has wished it. He has intended that the reader's heart should run over with ruth for the undeserved fate of that wretched woman. And it does. She is pure as undriven snow. We know that at some time far back she loved and sinned, but it was done when we did not know her. We are not told so, but come to understand, by the wonderful power of the writer in conveying that which he never tells, that there has been no taint of foulness in her love, though there has been deep sin. He never even tells us why that letter A has been used, though the abominable word is burning in our ears from first to last. We merely see her with her child, bearing her lot with patience, seeking for no comfort, doing what good she can in her humble solitude by the work of her hands, pointed at from all by the finger of scorn, but the purest, the cleanest, the fairest also among women. She never dreams of supposing that she ought not to be regarded as vile, while the reader's heart glows with a longing to take her soft hand and lead her into some pleasant place where the world shall be pleasant and honest and kind to her. I can fancy a reader so loving the image of Hester Prynne as to find himself on the verge of treachery to the real Hester of flesh and blood who may have a claim upon him. Sympathy can not go beyond that; and yet the author deals with her in a spirit of assumed hardness, almost as though he assented to the judgment and the manner in which it was carried out. In this, however, there is a streak of that satire with which Hawthorne always speaks of the peculiar institutions of his own country. The worthy magistrates of Massachusetts are under his lash throughout the story, and so is the virtue of her citizens and the chastity of her matrons, which can take delight in the open shame of a woman whose sin has been discovered. Indeed, there is never a page written by Hawthorne not tinged by satire.

The fourth character is that of the child, Pearl. Here the author has, I think, given way to a temptation, and in doing so has not increased the power of his story. The temptation was, that Pearl should add a picturesque element by being an elf and also a charming child. Elf she is, but, being so, is incongruous with all else in the story, in which, unhuman as it is, there is nothing of the ghostlike, nothing of the unnatural. The old man becomes a fiend, so to say, during the process of the tale; but he is a man-fiend. And Hester becomes sublimated almost to divine purity; but she is still simply a woman. The minister is tortured beyond the power of human endurance; but neither do his sufferings nor his failure of strength adequate to support them come to him from any miraculous agency. But Pearl is miraculous, — speaking, acting, and thinking like an elf, — and is therefore, I think, a drawback rather than an aid. The desolation of the woman, too, would have been more perfect without the child. It seems as though the author's heart had not been hard enough to make her live alone; — as sometimes when you punish a child you can not drive from your face that gleam of love which shoots across your frown and mars its salutary effect.

Hatred, fear, and shame are the passions which revel through the book. To show how a man may so hate as to be content to sacrifice everything to his hatred; how another may fear so that, even though it be for the rescue of his soul, he can not bring himself to face the reproaches of the world; how a woman may bear her load of infamy openly before the eyes of all men, — this has been Hawthorne's object. And surely no author was ever more successful. The relentless purpose of the man, in which is exhibited no passion, in which there is hardly a touch of anger, is as fixed as the hand of Fate. No one in the town knew that the woman was his wife. She had never loved him. He had left her alone in the world. But she was his wife; and, as the injury had been done to him, the punishment should follow from his hands! When he finds out who the sinner was, he does not proclaim him and hold him up to disgrace; he does not crush the almost adored minister of the gospel by declaring the sinner's trespass. He simply lives with his enemy in the same house, attacking not the man's body, — to which, indeed, he acts as a wise physician, — but his conscience, till we see the wretch writhing beneath the treatment.

Hester sees it too, and her strength, which suffices for the bearing of her own misery, fails her almost to fainting as she understands the condition of the man she has loved. Then there is a scene, the one graceful and pretty scene in the book, in which the two meet, — the two who were lovers, — and dare for a moment to think that they can escape. They come together in a wood, and she flings away, but for a moment, the badge of her shame, and lets down the long hair which has been hidden under her cap, and shines out before the reader for once, — just for that once, — as a lovely woman. She counsels him to fly, to go back across the waters to the old home whence he had come, and seek for rest away from the cruelty of his tyrant. When he pleads that he has no strength left to him for such action, then she declares that she will go with him and protect him and minister to him and watch over him with her strength. Yes; this woman proposes that she will then elope with the partner of her former sin. But no idea comes across the reader's mind of sinful love. The poor wretch can not live without service, and she will serve him. Were it herself that was concerned, she would remain there in her solitude, with the brand of her shame still open upon her bosom. But he can not go alone, and she too will therefore go.

As I have said before, the old man discovers the plot, and crushes their hopes simply by declaring that he will also be their companion. Whether there should have been this gleam of sunshine in the story the critic will doubt. The parent who would be altogether like Solomon should not soften the sternness of his frown by any glimmer of parental softness. The extreme pain of the chronicle is mitigated for a moment. The reader almost fears that he is again about to enjoy the satisfaction of a happy ending. When the blackness and the rumbling thunder-claps and the beating hailstones of a mountain storm have burst with all their fearful glories on the wanderer among the Alps, though he trembles and is awe-struck and crouches with the cold, he is disappointed rather than gratified when a little space of blue sky shows itself for a moment through the clouds. But soon a blacker mantle covers the gap, louder and nearer comes the crash, heavier fall the big drops till they seem to strike him to the bone. The storm is awful, majestic, beautiful; — but is it not too pitiless? So it is with the storm which bursts over that minister's head when the little space of blue has vanished from the sky.

But through all this intensity of suffering, through this blackness of narrative, there is ever running a vein of drollery. As Hawthorne himself says, "a lively sense of the humorous again stole in among the solemn phantoms of her thought." He is always laughing at something with his weird, mocking spirit. The very children when they see Hester in the streets are supposed to speak of her in this wise: "Behold, verily, there is the woman of the scarlet letter. Come, therefore, and let us fling mud at her." Of some religious book he says, "It must have been a work of vast ability in the somniferous school of literature." "We must not always talk in the market-place of what happens to us in the forest," says even the sad mother to her child. Through it all there is a touch of burlesque, — not as to the suffering of the sufferers, but as to the great question whether it signifies much in what way we suffer, whether by crushing sorrows or little stings. Who would not sooner be Prometheus than a yesterday's tipsy man with this morning's sick-headache? In this way Hawthorne seems to ridicule the very woes which he expends himself in depicting.

W. D. Howells

Hawthorne's Hester Prynne

There had been among the friendlier prophets overseas a vague expectation that the genuine American fiction, when it came, would be somehow aesthetically responsive to our vast continental spaces and the mighty forces that were taming the forests and prairies, the lakes and rivers, to the use of man. But when it came, the American fiction which owed nothing to English models differed from English fiction in nothing so much as its greater refinement, its subtler beauty, and its delicate perfection of form. While Dickens was writing in England, Hawthorne was writing in America; and for all the ostensible reasons the romances of Hawthorne ought to have been rude, shapeless, provisional, the novels of Dickens ought to have been fastidiously elect in method and material and of the last scrupulosity in literary finish. That is, they ought to have been so, if the obvious inferences from an old civilization ripened in its native air, and the same civilization so newly conditioned under alien skies that it seemed essentially new, were the right inferences. But there were some facts which such hasty conclusions must have ignored: chiefly the fact that the first impulse of a new artistic life is to escape from

From *Heroines of Fiction* (New York, 1901), I, 161-174.

crude conditions; and subordinately the fact that Hawthorne was writing to and from a sensitiveness of nerve in the English race that it had never known in its English home. We need not deny the greatness of Dickens in order to feel a patriotic content in the reflection that he represented English fiction in his time, and Hawthorne represented American fiction, as with the same implications Carlyle represented English thought and Emerson American thought.

I

Apart from the racial differences of the two writers, there was the widest possible difference of ideal in Dickens and Hawthorne; the difference between the romanticist and the romantic, which is almost as great as that between the romantic and the realistic. Romance, as in Hawthorne, seeks the effect of reality in visionary conditions; romanticism, as in Dickens, tries for a visionary effect in actual conditions. These different ideals eventuated with Hawthorne in characters being, doing, and suffering as vitally as any we have known in the world; with Dickens in types, outwardly of our every-day acquaintance, but inwardly moved by a single propensity and existing to justify in some fantastic excess the attribution of their controlling quality. In their mystical world, withdrawn afar from us in the past, or apart from us in anomalous conditions, the characters of Hawthorne speak and act for themselves, and from an authentic individuality compact of good and evil; in times, terms, and places analogous to those in which actual men have their being, the types of Dickens are always speaking for him, in fulfilment of a mechanical conception and a rigid limitation of their function in the drama. They are, in every sense, *parts*, and Hawthorne's creations are *persons*, rounded, whole. This fact appears in what has already been shown of Dickens, and it will appear concerning Hawthorne from any critical study of his romances.

II

There is, of course, a choice in Hawthorne's romances, and I myself prefer "The Blithedale Romance" and "The Scarlet Letter" to "The Marble Faun" and "The House of the Seven Gables." The last, indeed, I have found as nearly tiresome as I could find anything of Hawthorne's. I do not think it is censuring it unjustly to say that it seems the expansion of a short-story motive to the dimensions of a novel; and the slight narrative in which the concept is nursed with

whimsical pathos to the limp end, appears sometimes to falter, and
alarms the sympathetic reader at other times with the fear of an
absolute lapse. The characters all lack the vitality which the author
gives the people of his other books. The notion of the hapless Clifford
Pyncheon, who was natured for happiness and beauty, but was fated
to such a hard and ugly doom, is perhaps too single for the realization of a complete personality; and poor old Hepzibah, his sister, is
of scarcely more sufficient material. They move dim, forlorn wraiths
before the fancy, and they bring only such proofs of their reality as
ghosts seen by others can supply. The careful elaboration with which
they are studied seems only to render them more doubtful, and there
is not much in the pretty, fresh-hearted little Phoebe Pyncheon, or
her lover Holgrave, with all his generous rebellion against the obses-
sion of the present by the past, to render the central figures con-
vincing. Hawthorne could not help giving form to his work, but as
nearly as any work of his could be so "The House of the Seven
Gables" is straggling. There is at any rate no great womanly presence to pull it powerfully together, and hold it in the beautiful unity
characteristic of "The Blithedale Romance" and "The Scarlet Letter." What solidarity it has is in the simple Salem circumstance of
the story, where the antique Puritanic atmosphere merges with the
modern air in a complexion of perennial provinciality.

From the first there is no affectation of shadowy uncertainty in
the setting of the great tragedy of "The Scarlet Letter." As nearly
as can be, the scenes of the several events are ascertained, and are
identified with places in actual Boston. With a like inward sense of
strong reality in his material, and perhaps compelled to its expression by that force in the concept, each detail of the drama, in motive,
action, and character, is substantiated, so that from first to last it
is visible, audible, tangible. From Hester Prynne in her prison—
before she goes out to stand with her unlawful child in her arms and
the scarlet letter on her breast before the Puritan magistracy and
ministry and people, and be charged by the child's own father, as
her pastor, to give him up to like ignominy — to Hester Prynne,
kneeling over her dying paramour, on the scaffold, and mutely help-
ing him to own his sin before all that terrible little world, there is
the same strong truth beating with equal pulse from the core of the
central reality, and clothing all its manifestations in the forms of
credible, of indisputable personality.

In its kind the romance remains sole, and it is hard to see how
it shall ever be surpassed, or even companioned. It is not without
faults, without quaint foibles of manner which strike one oddly in

the majestic movement of the story; but with the exception of the love-child or sin-child, Pearl, there is no character, important or unimportant, about which you are asked to make believe: they are all there to speak and act for themselves, and they do not need the help of your fancy. They are all of a verity so robust that if one comes to declare Hester chief among them, it is with instant misgivings for the right of her secret paramour, Arthur Dimmesdale, and her secret husband, Roger Chillingworth, to that sorrowful supremacy. A like doubt besets the choice of any one moment of her history as most specific, most signal. Shall it be that dread moment on the pillory, when she faces the crowd with her child in her arms, and her lover adjures her to name its father, while her old husband on the borders of the throng waits and listens?

The Rev. Mr. Dimmesdale bent his head, in silent prayer, as it seemed, and then came forward. "Hester Prynne," said he, leaning over the balcony and looking down steadfastly into her eyes, . . . "if thou feelest it to be for thy soul's peace, and that thy earthly punishment will thereby be made more effectual to salvation, I charge thee to speak out the name of thy fellow-sinner and fellow-sufferer! Be not silent from any mistaken pity and tenderness for him; for, believe me, Hester, though he were to step down from a high place, and stand there beside thee, on thy pedestal of shame, yet better were it so, than to hide a guilty heart through life. . . . Heaven hath granted thee an open ignominy, that thereby thou mayest work out an open triumph over the evil within thee, and the sorrow without. Take heed how thou deniest to him — who, perchance, hath not the courage to grasp it for himself — the bitter, but wholesome, cup that is now presented to thy lips!" The young pastor's voice was tremulously sweet, rich, deep, and broken. The feeling that it so evidently manifested, rather than the direct purport of the words, caused it to vibrate within all hearts, and brought the listeners into one accord of sympathy. Even the poor baby, at Hester's bosom, was affected by the same influence; for it directed its hitherto vacant gaze towards Mr. Dimmesdale, and held up its little arms, with a half-pleased, half-plaintive murmur. . . . Hester shook her head. "Woman, transgress not beyond the limits of Heaven's mercy!" cried the Rev. Mr. Wilson, more harshly than before. . . . "Speak out the name! That, and thy repentance, may avail to take the scarlet letter off thy breast." "Never!" replied Hester Prynne, looking, not at Mr. Wilson, but into the deep and troubled eyes of the younger clergyman. "It is too deeply branded. Ye cannot take it off. And would that I might endure his agony, as well as mine!" "Speak, woman!" said another voice, coldly and sternly, proceeding from the

crowd about the scaffold. "Speak; and give your child a father!"
"I will not speak!" answered Hester, turning pale as death, but
responding to his voice, which she too surely recognized. "And my
child must seek a heavenly Father; she shall never know an earthly
one!" "She will not speak!" murmured Mr. Dimmesdale, who,
leaning over the balcony, with his hand upon his heart, had awaited
the result of his appeal. He now drew back, with a long respiration.
"Wondrous strength and generosity of a woman's heart! She will
not speak!"

III

One could hardly read this aloud without some such gasp and
catch as must have been in the minister's own breath as he spoke.
Yet piercing as the pathos of it is, it wants the ripened richness of
anguish, which the passing years of suffering bring to that meeting
between Hester Prynne and Arthur Dimmesdale in the forest, when
she tells him that his physician and closest companion is her husband, and that Chillingworth's subtlety has divined the minister's
relation to herself and her child. The reader must go to the book
itself for a full comprehension of the passage, but no one can fail of
its dramatic sense who recalls that Hester has by this time accustomed the little Puritan community to the blazon of her scarlet
letter, and in her lonely life of usefulness has conciliated her fellow-
townsfolk almost to forgiveness and forgetfulness of her sin. She has
gone in and out among them, still unaccompanied, but no longer
unfriended, earning her bread with her needle and care of the sick,
and Dimmesdale has held aloof from her like the rest, except for
their one meeting by midnight, when he stands with her and their
child upon the scaffold, and in that ghastly travesty forecasts the
union before the people which forms the catastrophe of the tremendous story.

In certain things "The Scarlet Letter," which was the first of
Hawthorne's romances, is the modernest and maturest. The remoteness of the time and the strangeness of the Puritan conditions autho-
rize that stateliness of the dialogue which he loved. The characters
may imaginably say "methinks" and "peradventure," and the other
things dear to the characters of the historical romancer; the narrator
himself may use an antiquated or unwonted phrase in which he finds
color, and may eschew the short-cuts and informalities of our actual
speech, without impeaching himself of literary insincerity. In fact,
he may heighten by these means the effect he is seeking; and if he

will only keep human nature strongly and truly in mind, as Hawthorne does in "The Scarlet Letter," we shall gratefully allow him
a privilege which may or may not be law. Through the veil of the
quaint parlance, and under the seventeenth-century costuming, we
see the human heart beating there the same as in our own time and
in all times, and the antagonistic motives working which have gov-
erned human conduct from the beginning and shall govern it forever,
world without end.

Hester Prynne and Arthur Dimmesdale are no mere types of open
shame and secret remorse. It is never concealed from us that he was
a man whose high and pure soul had its strongest contrast in the
nature

"Mixt with cunning sparks of hell,"

in which it was tabernacled for earth. It is still less hidden that,
without one voluntary lure or wicked art, she was of a look and make
to win him with the love that was their undoing. "He was a person
of a very striking aspect, with a wide, lofty, and impending brow;
large, brown, melancholy eyes, and a mouth which, unless he com-
pressed it, was apt to be tremulous. . . . The young woman was tall,
with a figure of perfect elegance on a large scale. She had dark and
abundant hair, so glossy that it threw off the sunshine with a gleam,
and a face which, besides being beautiful from the regularity of
feature and richness of complexion, had the impressiveness belonging to a marked brow and deep black eyes. She was ladylike, too,
after the manner of the feminine gentility of those days; characterized by a certain state and dignity, rather than by the delicate, eva-
nescent, and indescribable grace which is now recognized as its
indication." They were both of their time and place, materially as
well as spiritually; their lives were under the law, but their natures
had once been outside it, and might be again. The shock of this
simple truth can hardly be less for the witness, when, after its slow
and subtle evolution, it is unexpectedly flashed upon him, than it
must have been for the guilty actors in this drama, when they recognize that, in spite of all their open and secret misery, they are still
lovers, and capable of claiming for the very body of their sin a species
of justification.

We all know with what rich but noiseless preparation the consummate artist sets the scene of his most consummate effect; and
how, when Hester and Pearl have parted with Roger Chillingworth
by the shore, and then parted with each other in the forest, the
mother to rest in the shadow of the trees, and the child to follow

her fancies in play, he invokes the presence of Arthur Dimmesdale, as it were, silently, with a waft of the hand.

Slowly as the minister walked, he had almost gone by before Hester Prynne could gather voice enough to attract his observation. At length, she succeeded. "Arthur Dimmesdale!" she said, faintly at first; then louder, but hoarsely, "Arthur Dimmesdale!" "Who speaks?" answered the minister. . . . He made a step nigher, and discovered the scarlet letter. "Hester! Hester Prynne!" said he. "Is it thou? Art thou in life?" "Even so!" she answered. "In such life as has been mine these seven years past! And thou, Arthur Dimmesdale, dost thou yet live?" . . . So strangely did they meet, in the dim wood, that it was like the first encounter, in the world beyond the grave, of two spirits who had been intimately connected in their former life, but now stood coldly shuddering, in mutual dread; as not yet familiar with their state nor wonted to the companionship of disembodied beings. . . . It was with fear, and tremulously, and, as it were, by a slow, reluctant necessity, that Arthur Dimmesdale put forth his hand, chill as death, and touched the chill hand of Hester Prynne. The grasp, cold as it was, took away what was dreariest in the interview. They now felt themselves, at least, inhabitants of the same sphere. Without a word more spoken — neither he nor she assuming the guidance, but with an unexpected consent — they glided back into the shadow of the woods, whence Hester had emerged, and sat down on the heap of moss where she and Pearl had before been sitting. . . . "Hester," said he, "hast thou found peace?" She smiled drearily, looking down upon her bosom. "Hast thou?" she asked. "None!—nothing but despair!" he answered. "What else could I look for, being what I am, and leading such a life as mine?" . . . "The people reverence thee," said Hester. "And surely thou workest good among them. Doth this bring thee no comfort?" "More misery, Hester! — only the more misery!" answered the clergyman, with a bitter smile. . . . "Had I one friend — or were it my worst enemy — to whom, when sickened with the praises of all other men, I could daily betake myself, and be known as the vilest of all sinners, methinks my soul might keep itself alive thereby. Even thus much of truth would save me! But, now, it is all falsehood! — all emptiness! all death!" Hester Prynne looked into his face, but hesitated to speak. Yet, uttering his long-restrained emotions so vehemently as he did, his words here offered her the very point of circumstance in which to interpose what she came to say. She conquered her fears, and spoke. "Such a friend as thou hast even now wished for," said she, "with whom to weep over thy sin, thou hast in me, the partner of it!" — Again she hesitated, but brought out the words with an effort. — "Thou hast long had such an enemy, and dwellest with him, under the same roof!" The minister started to his feet, gasping for breath, and clutching at his heart, as if he would have torn it out of his bosom. "Ha! What sayest thou!" cried he. "An enemy! And under my own roof! What mean you?" . . . "O Arthur," cried she, "forgive me! In all things else I have striven to be true! Truth was the one virtue which I might have held fast, and did hold fast, through all extremity; save when thy good — thy life — thy fame — were put in question! Then I consented to a deception. But a lie is never good, even though death threaten on the other side! Dost thou not see what I would say? That old man! — the physician! — he whom they call Roger Chillingworth! — he was my husband!" The minister looked at her for an instant, with all that violence of passion which — intermixed, in more shapes than one, with his higher, purer, softer qualities — was, in fact, the portion of him which the Devil claimed, and through which he sought to win the rest. Never was there a blacker or a fiercer frown than Hester now encountered. For the brief space that it lasted, it was a dark transfiguration. But his character had been so much enfeebled by suffering, that even its lower energies were incapable of more than a temporary struggle. He sank down on the ground, and buried his face in his hands. . . . "O Hester Prynne, thou little, little knowest all the horror of this thing! And the shame! — the indelicacy! — the horrible ugliness of this exposure of a sick and guilty heart to the very eye that would gloat over it! Woman, woman, thou are accountable for this! I cannot forgive thee!" "Thou shalt forgive me!" cried Hester flinging herself on the fallen leaves beside him. "Let God punish. Thou shalt forgive!" With sudden and desperate tenderness, she threw her arms around him, and pressed his head against her bosom; little caring though his cheek rested on the scarlet letter. He would have released himself, but strove in vain to do so. Hester would not set him free, lest he should look her sternly in the face. All the world had frowned on her — for seven long years had it frowned upon this lonely woman — and still she bore it all, nor even once turned away her firm, sad eyes. Heaven, likewise, had frowned upon her, and she had not died. But the frown of this pale, weak, sinful, and sorrow-stricken man was what Hester could not bear and live! "Wilt thou yet forgive me?" she repeated, over and over again. "Wilt thou not frown? Wilt thou forgive?" "I do forgive you, Hester." replied the minister, at length, with a deep utterance, out of an abyss of sadness, but no anger. "I freely forgive you now. May God forgive us both! We are not, Hester, the worst sinners in the world. There is one worse than even the polluted priest! That old man's revenge has been blacker than my sin! He has violated, in cold blood, the sanctity of a human heart. Thou and I, Hester, never did so!" "Never, never!" whispered she. "What we did had a consecration of its own. We felt it so! We said so to each other!

Hast thou forgotten it?" "Hush, Hester!" said Arthur Dimmesdale,
rising from the ground. "No; I have not forgotten!" . . . "Thou must
dwell no longer with this man," said Hester, slowly and firmly. "Thy
heart must be no longer under his evil eye!" "It were far worse than
death!" replied the minister. "But how to avoid it? What choice
remains to me? Shall I lie down again on these withered leaves,
where I cast myself when thou didst tell me what he was? Must I
sink down there, and die at once?" "Alas, what a ruin has befallen
thee!" said Hester, with the tears gushing into her eyes. "Wilt thou
die for very weakness? There is no other cause." "The judgment of
God is on me," answered the conscience-stricken priest. "It is too
mighty for me to struggle with!" "Heaven would show mercy," re-
joined Hester, "hadst thou but the strength to take advantage of it."
"Be thou strong for me," answered he. "Advise me what to do." "Is
the world, then, so narrow?" exclaimed Hester Prynne, fixing her deep
eyes on the minister's, and instinctively exercising a magnetic power
over a spirit so shattered and subdued that it could hardly hold itself
erect. "Whither leads yonder forest track? . . . Deeper it goes, and
deeper into the wilderness, less plainly to be seen at every step, until,
some few miles hence, the yellow leaves will show no vestige of the
white man's tread. . . . Is there not shade enough in all this boundless
forest to hide thy heart from the gaze of Roger Chillingworth?" "Yes,
Hester; but only under the fallen leaves," replied the minister, with a
sad smile. "Then there is the broad pathway of the sea!" continued
Hester. "It brought thee hither. If thou choose, it will bear thee back
again." . . . "O Hester!" cried Arthur Dimmesdale, in whose eyes a
fitful light, kindled by her enthusiasm, flashed up and died away,
"thou tellest of running a race to a man whose knees are tottering
beneath him! I must die here! There is not the strength or courage
left me to venture into the wide, strange, difficult world, alone!" . . .
"Thou shalt not go alone!" answered she, in a deep whisper. Then, all
was spoken.

There is a greatness in this scene which is unmatched, I think, in
the book, and, I was almost ready to say, out of it. At any rate, I
believe we can find its parallel only in some of the profoundly impas-
sioned pages of the Russian novelists who, casting aside all the common adjuncts of art, reveal us to ourselves in the appeal from their
own naked souls. Hawthorne had another ideal than theirs, and a
passing love of style, and the meaning of the music of words. For
the most part, he makes us aware of himself, of his melancholy grace
and sombre power; we feel his presence in every passage, however
deeply, however occultly, dramatic; he overshadows us, so that we
touch and see through him. But here he is almost out of it; only a

few phrases of comment, so fused in feeling with the dialogue that they are like the voice of a chorus, remind us of him.

It is the most exalted instant of the tragedy, it is the final evolution of Hester Prynne's personality. In this scene she dominates by virtue of whatever is womanly and typical in her, and no less by what is personal and individual. In what follows, she falls like Dimmesdale and Chillingworth under the law of their common doom, and becomes a figure on the board where for once she seemed to direct the game.

In all fiction one could hardly find a character more boldly, more simply, more quietly imagined. She had done that which in the hands of a feeble or falser talent would have been suffered or made to qualify her out of all proportion and keeping with life. But her transgression does not qualify her, as transgression never does unless it becomes habit. She remains exterior and superior to it, a life of other potentialities, which in her narrow sphere she fulfils. What she did has become a question between her and her Maker, who apparently does not deal with it like a Puritan. The obvious lesson of the contrasted fates of Dimmesdale and herself is that to own sin is to disown it, and that it cannot otherwise be expropriated and annulled. Yet, in Hester's strong and obstinate endurance of her punishment there is publicity but not confession; and perhaps there is a lesson of no slighter meaning in the inference that ceasing to do evil is, after all, the most that can be asked of human nature. Even that seems to be a good deal, and in "The Scarlet Letter" it is a stroke of mastery to show that it is not always ours to cease to do evil, but that in extremity we need the help of the mystery "not ourselves, that makes for righteousness," and that we may call Chance or that we may call God, but that does not change in essence or puissance whatever name we give it.

4. Revival and Reassessment

John E. Hart

"The Scarlet Letter"— One Hundred Years After

Exactly twenty-five years after he had left Bowdoin to become a writer, Hawthorne published his first successful novel, *The Scarlet Letter*. Its popular appeal had enabled its creator to open "an intercourse with the world," and to achieve the fame that the writer-hero Fanshawe had dreamed of in that slight first novel, published in 1828. As a way of re-examining *The Scarlet Letter*, we might read it as symbolic action and say that it was doing something for Hawthorne that it was doing for no one else. To relate the pattern of Hawthorne's life to the attitudes and actions of the characters in the novel is to discover that they represent different sides of his own personality. Through them he explores the necessity of Art as a way of expiating his feeling of guilt towards his Past, as well as the relationship of the isolated individual to the outside world.

Certainly Hawthorne's feeling of solitude produced a conflict in his mind, a mental state akin to guilt, that was, as Newton Arvin has pointed out, to become a central problem in the stories and novels. Deeply rooted in his Past, Hawthorne's feeling was dualistic in

From the *New England Quarterly*, XXIII (September 1950), 381-395. Reprinted by permission of the publisher and the author.

nature. When he went to Raymond, Maine, with his mother, he remembered that here in this "fine wild solitary place" he spent some of the happiest moments of his life, but that here also he acquired the "cursed habits of solitude." Habituated by the early life with his mother, and by a three years' confinement while convalescing from a foot injury and a temporary lameness, Hawthorne was hardly trained to deal with a world of computations and accounts when he went to work in his uncle's stagecoach business in Salem. He wrote his mother: "No man can be a Poet and a bookkeeper at the same time."

The twelve solitary years that Hawthorne spent in Salem must be considered only as a temporary withdrawal for a purpose: he wanted to become a writer, and as a writer, he wanted fame and the acceptance of his stories by the public. If Hawthorne suffered a feeling of guilt from his Past and his solitude, he saw both as a necessary evil to artistic success. As we shall see in *The Scarlet Letter*, it was not isolation itself that produced guilt; rather, it was the feeling of frustration at having chosen Art as a way of life, at being a person of imagination and sensibility. It was the awareness of a world that seemed to emphasize material values rather than human values. Hawthorne's problem was complex and highly personal: how could he convert the particular ingredients of his experience into a successful work of Art that would expiate his feeling of guilt toward the Past, and, at the same time, establish himself as a successful writer? To answer this question is to cut through the wealth of symbols which, in a sense, conceal the stated problems, yet, at the same time, reveal the artistry of his accomplishment.

The key to understanding the symbolic action of *The Scarlet Letter* lies with the use of the "shadow" metaphor. In searching for what Hawthorne associates with the word, we might look for its use elsewhere to establish a pattern of meaning. In "The Devil in Manuscript," the writers says:

> I am surrounding myself with shadows, which bewilder me, by aping the realities of life. They have drawn me aside from the beaten path of the world, and led me into a strange sort of solitude—a solitude in the midst of men—where nobody wishes for what I do, nor thinks nor feels as I do.

In a letter to Sophia Peabody, his fiancée, we find further associations:

Thou only hast revealed me to myself; for without thy aid, my best knowledge of myself would have been merely to know my own shadow. . . . Indeed we are but shadows . . . till the heart is touched. That touch creates us. . . .

We note that the "shadows" have a magnetic power. They induce solitude and an unreal attitude and thus prevent communication with an audience. But "shadows" have also given a partial understanding of oneself and have really led to the touch that creates with compassion and understanding. As Ellen, the heroine of *Fanshawe*, might have been the tie that connected the writer-hero to the world, so Sophia seems actually to have become what was a necessary partner to the act of creation. Hawthorne might have been thinking in both artistic and sexual terms; however, it is his exploration of the former as a way of expiating the Past that shall chiefly concern us here. *The Scarlet Letter*, seen in terms of the function of Art, appears to be the pivotal writing of Hawthorne's career.

Returning to the Past, some two hundred years previous, for the scene of action, Hawthorne introduces the use of a particular set of symbols. We see Hester Prynne, the heroine, for the first time as she emerges from the prison, "the black flower of civilized society," from the shadows, "the gray twilight of a dungeon." Just as the prison confines the drab-garbed Hester, relieved only by the scarlet "A," "so artistically done, and with so much fertility and gorgeous luxuriance of fancy," so does the prison overshadow the rosebush, which serves "to symbolize some sweet moral blossom . . . or relieve the darkening close of a tale of human frailty and sorrow." To show how the words have been linked together, we can make the following listings:

black flower	rosebush
shadows	Scarlet A
dungeon	artistry, fertility, fancy
forest	moral blossom

If the above lists show what goes with what, the symbols, at the same time, carry implicit dichotomous attitudes, which we will explore later. It is clear that the sides are in conflict, and that Hester's actions have embodied attitudes representative of both. Actually, as "shadows" connote imprisonment and solitude, so the scarlet letter implies a way out.

What blooms about Hester as she emerges from the prison is the scarlet letter. It has "the effect of a spell"; it takes "her out of the ordinary relations with humanity" and encloses "her in a sphere by herself." The Puritan society sees the letter in a different light; it represents a symbol of guilt, the individual's violation of the moral code. Probably because she is partly Puritan also, Hester feels guilty too; therefore, she cannot deal with the "leaden inflicting glances" of the onlookers. She dreams of her Past:

> Reminiscences the most trifling and immaterial, passages of infancy and school days, . . . came swarming back upon her. . . . Possibly it was an instinctive device of her spirit, to relieve itself, by the exhibition of these phantasmagoric forms, from the cruel weight and hardness of the reality.

But Hester's position on the scaffold induces memory of an unpleasant Past as well. She recalls her poverty-stricken home in England, her mother's remonstrances, the "scholar-like visage" of her husband, the "stern regards" of these Puritans. Consequently, she realizes now that her infant and shame are real, that her Past is inescapable. Looking at the crowd, she sees her husband, Roger Chillingworth, standing among them. Her Past is not phantom-like, but real.

It is this dualistic power of the Past that motivates Hester's action. Although she might have tried hiding her identity in some new place, she withdraws to the outskirts of the little town, and lives in isolation. As Hawthorne declares,

> there is a fatality, a feeling so irresistible and inevitable that it has the force of doom, which almost invariably compels human beings to linger around and haunt, ghost-like, the spot where some great and marked event has given the color to their lifetime. . . .

Like the rosebush at the prison door, the sin is the root which Hester has "struck into the soil," but, like the rosebush, the sin, although binding her to an isolated fate forever, is a new birth, which helps to assimilate the wild joy of her nature with her new home.

Hester's Past functions for her as Hawthorne's did for him. If he had found solitude to be a cursed habit, he had, at the same time, found it necessary for the practice of his craft, which, in turn, provided an outlet for his imagination. This double attitude towards the Past is best expressed by Holgrave in *The House of the Seven Gables*. Holgrave is an artist, who dwells in the old house, "expressive of that odious and abominable Past," so that he "may know the better how to hate it." As "one method of throwing off" Maule's curse [the Past], he will "put an incident of the Pyncheon family history . . . into the form of a legend, and . . . publish it in a magazine." We might think of the experience which Hawthorne's Past had given him as a commodity for sale, and of his imagination and writing ability as a mode of peddling that commodity. If the writer Hawthorne had isolated himself with an unmarketable product, he had found in it the same kind of therapeutic value that, as we shall soon see, Hester had found in the scarlet letter.

What distinguishes Hester from her Puritan neighbors, and what saves her from her fate, is her creative ability. Living under a "mystic shadow of suspicion," she turns to her art of needlework, of which the scarlet "A" is a "specimen of her delicate and imaginative skill." With the Puritans this addition of "spiritual adornment of human ingenuity" to their fabrics was reserved for the "official state of men assuming the reins of power." From the standpoint of function, power is exactly what the embroidery gives Hester—power and a feeling of joy. Hawthorne indicates (as in the commentary on the pageantry of the Election Day) that the Puritans saw any expression of joy as a cardinal sin. The needlework may express, as well as soothe, Hester's passions, but such an act is, to her own Puritan nature as to the Puritans themselves, like piling sin on sin. If her "art" relieves her guilt endured in solitude, what will save her publicly from the greater sin of having expressed through Art the very emotions that got her into trouble? Although she always exhibits her guilt by wearing the letter, she continues to endure the burden of having tried to "relieve" that guilt through Art and through little Pearl, who is the living embodiment of all the scarlet letter stands for. Hester's mode of life still implies the idea of penance, the idea that there is a price to pay.

In terms of characters that price is Pearl. Part of the function of her character, which is developed later in the story as expressing part of Hawthorne's attitude, lies in her relationship to the Past. Pearl "had not been made at all, but had been plucked by her mother off the bush of wild roses that grew by the prison door." As "the outgrowth of her mother's brain," she lacks "reference and adaptation to the world into which she was born." In her gorgeously embroidered robes, she possesses all the power, joy, passion, and imaginative qualities associated with the scarlet "A." She has an "ever-creative spirit." She is lawless. She moves in a "circle of radiance." She dances in the sunshine, never in the shadows.

From the metaphors used to describe Pearl, we see that through her Hawthorne defines an attitude which accepts the creative spirit as a necessary part of man's life. Cut off from the roots of the Past, Pearl can judge action (precocious child that she is) not according to previous moral standards, but according to the amount of truth demonstrated to her. She acts always as her skeptical and innocent nature dictates. But, having inherited the "enmity and passion . . . of Hester's heart," the born outcast appears to the little Puritans as an unearthly child in league with witchcraft. Obviously, the society in which she lives has no capacity for understanding her.

Hawthorne seems to have drawn the attitudes expressed by these two characters from his own experience. As Hester is able to save herself in part through her creative abilities so Hawthorne can use his writing to redeem his hatred for the Past. He can throw off the guilt felt towards his Puritan ancestors, towards his isolation from society, even, perhaps, towards his own mother. If we substitute Art for the scarlet letter, we can see that Hawthorne was using it, like Hester, to open "an intercourse with the world." Pearl, then, might symbolize what Hawthorne as artist would wish to become, what art itself must do to save an individual from shadowy solitude, so that he can move towards the attitude of the "creative spirit." Pearl's character throughout the story is developed from the attitude that she has nothing to conceal.

If lack of concealment motivates Pearl's actions, the reverse is true of those of Roger Chillingworth. Coming to Boston under a pseudonym, he obviously has something to hide, something that a renaming might either destroy or, at least, conceal. It is his Past, and that Past has to do with Hester. Running into her on the scaffold, he must have been as disconcerted as she. If he can forgive her present ignominious position, he cannot forgive her partner, who has betrayed her as he himself once did. Misshapen at birth, he has tried to delude himself "with the idea that intellectual gifts might veil physical deformity in a young girl's fantasy!" He had married Hester because his heart was "lonely and chill." He had betrayed her youth "into a false and unnatural relation" with decay. His guilt, greater even than Hester's, is that of a diseased mind which puts its complete hope in intellect, not passion, and which leads to decay, not growth and understanding.

Chillingworth expresses Hawthorne's attitude toward people who rely solely on intellect. As a man who values "intelligence and learning" above all, Chillingworth is like those men who have "materialized their faculties" and have "lost the spiritual view of existence amid the intricacies of that wondrous mechanism," the human frame. Such men are not devoid of emotion; rather, their emotion is turned to destructive purposes. As with the Puritans, whose repressed feelings have festered into a passion that pries into other people's hearts—as in the case of Ethan Brand, so Chillingworth's emotions are manifested as hatred. Using a diseased Puritan culture as background, Hawthorne has put the right agent in the right scene. Chillingworth's actions can go undetected in a society characterized by fraud and decay as Hester's can not. Without violating any moral code of society, he can pursue punitive measures in being his brother's—if not his wife's—keeper. The destruction of Hester's lover through revenge, then, only conceals Chillingworth's real motive of trying to redeem his own guilty conscience, which is, of course, actually beyond redemption.

What Chillingworth does and believes tells more about Hawthorne than is readily apparent. We remember that Hawthorne's own temporary lameness had enforced a solitude in which he read and studied, and that the habits of solitude, which he had formed, prevented his understanding the men in the stagecoach and Custom House offices. We also remember that his mother and sister Elizabeth had questioned his marriage to Sophia, and that, although he felt tender towards his mother, there had been, "ever since . . . boyhood, a sort of coldness of intercourse between" them. We remember, further, that his first novel and short stories had appeared without signature or under a pseudonym, as if, like the physician, he wanted to hide something. It was his Past, which he had come to hate. He was a failure in a world where there was little recognition of his talents.

Hawthorne's feeling of hatred seems to be a kind of revenge for his own life, a revenge which sent him prying into his own heart like any good Puritan. From experience he began to see what might happen to him if he came to believe in only material values, and if he tried to disguise or control his creative spirit. Chillingworth represents that part of Hawthorne's Past which he was trying to "throw off."

The object of Chillingworth's search is, of course, the Reverend Arthur Dimmesdale, Hester's lover. A Puritan minister, he is scholarly, well read, eloquent in his religious fervor. His presence at Hester's "crucifixion" in the village square arouses no suspicion from the admiring Puritans, for Dimmesdale is really one of them. But there is something extraordinary about him. He has an apprehensive, a startled, a half-frightened look,—as of a being who felt himself quite astray and at a loss in the pathway of human existence, and could only be at ease in some seclusion of his own.

Like Hester and Chillingworth, he is a creature of solitude, but in terms of his individual self, his withdrawal has a positive effect:

> . . . he trod in the shadowy by-paths, and thus kept himself simple and childlike; coming forth, when occasion was, with a freshness, and fragrance, and dewy purity of thought, which as many people said, affected them like the speech of an angel.

Compare the above quotation with one from a letter that Hawthorne wrote to Sophia Peabody:

> I begin to understand why I was imprisoned so many years in this lonely chamber, and why I could never break through the viewless bolts and bars; for if I had sooner made my escape into the world, I should have grown hard and rough, and been covered with earthly dust, and my heart might have become callous by rude encounters with the multitude . . . , but living in solitude till the fulness of time was come, I still kept the dew of my youth and freshness of my heart.

Clearly, as the metaphors indicate, Dimmesdale represents Hawthorne's own feelings toward solitude.

Hawthorne is not, however, in complete sympathy with Dimmesdale: although the minister's act of withdrawal is sanctioned because it preserves his dewy purity of thought, what is it that has made him withdraw in the first place? As we know, he has, like Hester, violated the moral code of the Puritans. He has concealed his hypocrisy by his angelic speech and clerical garb. Hawthorne's criticism of his action is apparent: the minister has tried to atone for his physical passion by withdrawing from the world to a spiritual haven. Although he has, unlike Chillingworth, managed to keep his thought pure and fresh, rather than false and sterile, he must now deal with his hypocrisy. In the shadows of solitude, he has been quite safe with his own feeling of guilt. What Dimmesdale does not know is that a probing intellect is about to uncover his secret.

As the story unfolds, Chillingworth's function as a man of intellect is to seek revenge without exposing himself. His relationship to the minister is that of doctor to patient. Dimmesdale apparently has no cause for worry. Like that of any physician, Chillingworth's rôle is to cure the members of a sick society. The doctor is no fool. He knows the symptoms of a guilty man when he sees them. Dimmesdale studies too much; he fasts; he is concerned with duty; he is confined within the "iron framework" of his faith; his face is flushed; he puts his hand over his heart, as if to hide something. Chillingworth perceives that the minister is a man of "thought and imagination, a person of sensibility." To effect a cure, the old herb gatherer picks some "dark, flabby leaves," which, he explains, once grew from some hideous secret of the heart.

Actually that hideous secret of the heart, which the minister tries to hide, is his sexual passion, of which the flush, like the scarlet letter, is an outward manifestation. It is interesting to observe that Hawthorne uses the same metaphors to describe both: the scarlet "A," as we have seen, symbolizes artistry, fertility, the fancy found in Hester's make-up, the freshness of heart, the fragrance of Pearl's simplicity; likewise, the flush indicates freshness, fragrance, the dewy purity of thought, the acknowledgment that the minister is a creature of both thought and passion. Certainly, the flush bears the same relation to the minister's withdrawal that the scarlet letter does to Hester's. Under the aegis of solitude, both the letter and the flush afford a release for the individuals. From the standpoint of function, both are identical.

As Hester's embroidered "A" has magnetized the Puritan society with its magic, so the flush has given the minister a terrible, persuasive power. "The virgins of his church [grow] pale around him." They are partners in religious passion, and their public veneration tortures the young minister, although he has always desired the fame that veneration would bring. Actually, the virgins have made him aware of his passionate nature, and since he continues to conceal it, he is tortured by the realization that he has become a "pollution and a lie." As Hawthorne implies through his portrayal of the minister's relation to his congregation, society worships hypocrisy, not truth. But if Hawthorne accuses society of hypocrisy, his main accusation is against the individual in that society: ". . . above all things else, [the minister] loathed his miserable self!" Puritan that he was, he must do penance for his terrible guilt.

Like Hester on the scaffold, the minister turns to his Past for consolation: during his vigils, he sees visions, diabolical shapes, his father, his mother, and finally Hester and Pearl, who points an accusing finger at his breast. These visions become "the truest and most substantial things which the poor minister now dealt with." "The only truth that continued to give Mr. Dimmesdale a real existence on this earth was the anguish in his inmost soul, and the undissembled expression of it in his aspect." Torn between "the agony of heaven-defying guilt and vain repentance," the minister walks to the town square and ascends the steps of the scaffold. In the dark gray of midnight, "there was no peril of discovery." It is here that he invites little Pearl and Hester to join him. As they clasp hands, the minister feels a "tumultuous rush of new life, . . . pouring like a torrent into his heart." In a kind of ritual, the joining of the three outcasts has given a rebirth to the minister, but since the act is accomplished in the shadowy solitude, the effect is only temporary. As dawn approaches, the lawless chain is broken. Roger Chillingworth sees them and, by his insidious intellect, understands that his plan of revenge may be thwarted.

The character of Chillingworth is developed according to Hawthorne's conception of what happens to a man who relies too much on material values. Repressed by devoting himself for seven years to the torture of his victim, he has become a fiend. This fiend-like expression is now disguised by a smile, which plays him false and throws his blackness into greater relief. His mind has absorbed his evil intent, the effects of his physical deformity, the whole disease of the age. He has, we might say, absorbed in his visage the very evil which has corrupted the minister. His repressed emotions have become hatred, revealed only by a "glare of red light out of his eyes." Deformed in both appearance and intellect, the physician moves in shadow only. Yet it is this hatred in Chillingworth that arouses a similar feeling in Hester and causes her to act. She resolves to warn the minister of the old physician's purpose of exposing and thus destroying him.

To understand Hester's resolution is to understand her present relationship with society. Although the Puritans have continued to accept her noble deeds because she suffers the ignominious letter, she herself has changed. During the years, her "life had turned, in a great measure, from passion and feeling, to thought." As a result, she has ceased to battle with the public, has submitted to it uncomplainingly. As Hawthorne explains,

> It is remarkable that persons who speculate the most boldly often conform with the most perfect quietude to the external regulations of society. The thought suffices them, without investing itself in the flesh and blood of action.

Action, by all means. Independent thought is insufficient for Hester to redeem her relationship with Dimmesdale, that part of her Past which is still concealed from society. But there is an even more important result of her reliance on thought. The world is becoming more hostile towards little Pearl. Like her needlework, Pearl has given her great comfort in isolation, but what of her obligation to Pearl? Further, what of Pearl's relationship to society?

It is important to remember that Pearl is the living symbol of both sin and art. In terms of Hawthorne's self-scrutiny, she seems to embody the ambivalence of the double attitude: to her mother's solitude she has brought both joy and sorrow. In reality — as Hester has moved towards "thought" — Pearl's ever-creative spirit has become a greater burden to her mother as, we might suggest, Hawthorne's practice of his craft had become a greater burden to him. What Hawthorne seems to imply is that his solitary years were a kind of necessary evil, but that his being a man of sensitivity, passion, and creativeness was an even greater evil. It was not living in solitude that was a sin; rather it was his creative nature that demanded and needed to be revealed that put him at odds with society. Yet by the practice of a profession that society ignored, if not scorned, Hawthorne sought to achieve fame and position, to be thus recognized and accepted by that society.

With Pearl, then, lies the solution to the problem of sin, with all its connotations of pride, revenge, and hypocrisy. She is the only character that is morally and intellectually healthy. She is completely guiltless of the Past, because she has no Past. She operates by her own law and is, therefore, lawless from the stand-point of the Puritans. She is the only free agent because she need not conceal her true feelings from anyone. Metaphorically, she moves in truth and sunshine, rather than in guilt and sorrow.

When Pearl accompanies her mother to the forest — symbol of moral wilderness — to warn the minister of Chillingworth's plan of revenge, she flits like a bird in the bright sunshine. She sees that the sun does not love her mother. "I am but a child. It will not flee from me, for I wear nothing on my bosom yet!" As she dances, the sun becomes part of her "vivacity of spirit." Her actions are easily converted into the attitude towards society which Hawthorne felt. In a letter he wrote, his metaphors might very well be describing Pearl:

> How much mud and mire, how many pools of unclean water, how many slippery footsteps, and perchance heavy tumbles, might be avoided if one could tread but six inches above the crust of this world. Physically we cannot do this; our bodies cannot, but it seems

to me that our hearts and minds may keep themselves above moral mud puddles and other discomforts of the soul's pathway.

To understand Pearl is to realize that the individual must achieve detachment so that the heart and mind can achieve understanding. As a symbol of creativeness, Pearl is both sin and sanctity, for as the artist is damned to and by isolation, so isolation preserves the fertility of the imagination, the balance between heart and mind.

There is a further implication of creativeness. If sensitivity leads to truth and love, Hawthorne implies that it can also lead to falsity and hate. The introspection of Chillingworth and, to a lesser extent, that of Dimmesdale, aptly demonstrates what happens when that balance between heart and mind is not maintained. Hawthorne believed that sentiment was an inevitable and unavoidable part of his make-up: it was "probably assignable to the deep and aged roots" which his family had "stuck into the soil." Rooted to the Past, he had come to hate what it stood for, the power it had over him. Yet he believed that such a feeling could be overcome with experience. He wrote: "It contributes greatly towards a man's moral and intellectual health to be brought into habits of companionship with individuals unlike himself." It was the lesson he had learned at the Custom House. It was the lesson he had learned as a writer without an audience.

Pearl represents, then, the attitude towards which Hawthorne was moving when he wrote *The Scarlet Letter*. It is not until the final scene of the story, when the minister acknowledges his guilt in the village square, that Pearl runs and kisses him. Her tears, Hawthorne writes, "were the pledge that she would grow up amid human joy and sorrow, nor forever do battle with the world, but be a woman in it." Freedom consists not only in showing freely to the world; it also consists in realizing that love and hate are perhaps the same, and that "each renders one individual dependent for the food of his affections and spiritual life upon another."

In a romance that constitutes his most complete working out of a complex response to a very personal dilemma, Hawthorne has drawn his characters as different sides of his own personality. The metaphorical style "conceals" — as if it were a reflection of his disguise — the antagonism between intellect and passion, between the material and immaterial, the struggle between habit patterns of his life, one impelled towards concealing, the other towards revealing a double attitude towards the Past. Because he wanted to "throw off" this hatred for his Past, he had resolved to become a writer. As a keen observer of his own mind and heart, he had, prompted by his own experience, reached certain attitudes: he saw that to avenge his feelings by use of intellect was to decay as a Roger Chillingworth; to disguise those feelings through religion was to live the life of a hypocrite as a Reverend Mr. Dimmesdale; to reveal those feelings by relying wholly on himself as artist was to live always in solitude as a Hester Prynne. If he felt that his chosen profession were sinful when seen from the eyes of society, he also felt that it was purifying if seen from the eyes of the individual. If the practice of Art had driven him into solitude, his reaction to solitude had forced him into an acceptance of his world. He saw that Art was useless unless it was accepted by society. Like Pearl, only by showing freely both mind and heart to the world could he gain a release from the Past, success, fame. But more important, he could feel at home in his world; he could call his Custom House friends brethren.

Daniel G. Hoffman

Hester's Double Providence: The Scarlet Letter and the Green

I

Hawthorne seems never to mention the imagination without invoking images of supernatural power. In 'Feathertop' the imagination is compared to witchcraft, in 'The Snow Image' to magic, in 'The Devil in Manuscript' to demonism. Although invocation of the Muse was out of fashion when Hawthorne wrote his romances, in his prefaces he performed a somewhat similar rite. In each he attempts to define the nature of his imaginative faculty. And in each he sets forth the difficulties in the way of its exercise upon the materials of reality. These difficulties he felt to be especially acute in his American climate of rationality, skepticism, and literal-mindedness. The preface to *The Scarlet Letter* is no brief foreword, but the fifty-page sketch of 'The Custom-House.' Its primary reason for being is to lead the reader backwards in time, away from the dull commonplaceness of the present toward the past in which the imagination can illuminate reality with a glow

From *Form and Fable in American Fiction* (Copyright © Oxford University Press, 1961), pp. 169-186. Reprinted by permission.

like moonlight or firelight. What Hawthorne seeks is 'a neutral territory, somewhere between the real world and fairy-land, where the Actual and the Imaginary may meet, and each imbue itself with the nature of the other.' There, he says, 'Ghosts might enter . . . without affrighting us.'

Only by the exercise of psychological distance from fact could Hawthorne create his neutral territory. While in the Custom House, his imagination was but 'a tarnished mirror.' In bringing to life 'the figures with which I did my best to people it' he found the intermixture of the supernatural with the real an artistic necessity. For the very reason that the contemporary attitude toward art and its essential myths seemed typified by the scorn of Peter Hovendon (in 'The Artist of the Beautiful') or by the unfeeling insensitivity of the hardware merchant (in 'The Snow Image'), the creation of myth seemed all the more urgent to Hawthorne. One must question F. O. Matthiessen's judgment that 'Hawthorne . . . did not conceive of his work in any relation to myth. He did not seek for universal analogies, but gained his moral profundity by remaining strictly a provincial and digging where he was.'[1] At the lower levels of imaginative intensity his predilection towards myth is apparent enough. Granting that such juvenile books as *Tanglewood Tales*, *A Wonder Book*, and *Grandfather's Chair* were but hack work, we nonetheless observe that Hawthorne chose as his subjects the making plausible of Greek myths and, as in his early tales, the making mythical of Colonial history.

When we turn to Hawthorne's American romances we shall find that they are indeed conceived in relation to myths. Some of the mythic elements will be those which we have already discovered in his tales. In the romances as in the shorter fiction, his images of unfallen paganism, of the universal community of witchcraft, of the self-transforming native character, are combined with other elements not the results of provincial experience. Where these three themes had often furnished Hawthorne with the major concepts for his tales, in the romances they are more often used as ancillaries to the dominant tensions. They provide him with three culturally sanctioned traditions upon which to draw in delineating his characters and their symbolic roles.

In *The Scarlet Letter* the folklore of the supernatural is peculiarly appropriate to the development of Hawthorne's conflicts. The romance itself may be said to be based upon yet another myth, if

---

[1] *American Renaissance* (New York, 1941), pp. 630-31.

we may consider as myth the Puritan doctrine which it is the fate of Hester, Dimmesdale, and Chillingworth to test. In his re-creation of Puritan society in this book, Hawthorne, as we have already observed, takes pains to include superstition and witchcraft among the articles of popular belief. In fact the moral universe of *The Scarlet Letter* contains both the diabolical otherworld of 'Young Goodman Brown' and the pagan paradise of Merry Mount. These supernatural realms are metaphorically and inferentially significant, but the locale of the action, unlike that in these shorter tales, is literally the life of this world. Merry Mount was an Eden before the Fall, the Witches' Sabbath seemed a dream, but Governor Bellingham's Boston, with jail and scaffold at its very center, represents the actual world. It is just such a world through which the lovers expelled from Merry Mount would have to follow a 'difficult path,' though heaven be their destination.

The May-day paradise of Hester Prynne and Arthur Dimmesdale has been blasted and they expelled before the story of *The Scarlet Letter* begins. When we revisit the scene of what the Puritans called their sin but what the author terms their 'crime,' we are again in the forest. This was the site of both the Maypole and the witches' revels. The imagery of paganism and of witchcraft picks up these supernatural associations in *The Scarlet Letter*. Among a people to whom 'religion and law were almost identical,' superstition proves surprisingly nearer than dogma to spiritual truth.

While these uses of pagan and witchcraft belief are allusive and imagistic, there is yet a further role played by superstition in *The Scarlet Letter*. For his most characteristic device of style — which is to say, his way of looking at experience — Hawthorne took advantage of the folk tradition of the wonder. He makes the letter itself a supernatural providence; yet instead of evoking allegorical certitude it produces ambiguity on every side. Its significance is established by the conflicting testimony of several eye-witnesses. Popular tradition believes them all. Hawthorne's reliance upon the alternative interpretations which oral tradition gives to supernatural wonders proves to be a structural principle essential to his conception of *The Scarlet Letter*.

II

In Hawthorne's romance the scarlet letter itself serves as the controlling symbol of our thought, continually raising and defining problems which its inflicters did not acknowledge to exist. Those

Puritan judges, sincerely pious but tragically restricted in their understanding of the soul, are unwittingly guilty of a sin more grievous than Hester's own. For they have taken it into their prideful hearts to pass absolute judgment upon a fellow-being, and to construct, for the supposed benefit of their own holy community, a man-made remarkable providence in imitation of God's wonders. Recalling Increase Mather's definition of the genre, we recognize Hester's 'A' as among the 'Remarkable Judgements upon noted Sinners' which comprised one of the varieties of his *Illustrious Providences*.

But if the Puritans in Hawthorne's romance are unaware of their own pride in presuming to judge Hester as God judges her, we are enabled to see their inadequacies as the letter works its influence in ways they had not dreamed. Not only that, but God Himself has passed a 'Remarkable Judgement' upon Hester. This judgement His zealous communicants are too blind to recognize, although it is just as plainly visible as the ignominy with which they brand her. For the actual 'Remarkable Providence' which God has brought about as a living emblem of Hester's sin is revealed in the same opening scene in which we first see the scarlet letter. Hester appears on the scaffold bearing her child in her arms: it is soon manifest that in the allegorical scheme of this romance, Pearl='A.'

It is through its similitude with Pearl that the scarlet letter can become endowed with life. Indeed, it seems to have a life of its own, as we shall see, in which the letter changes its relationship to the other characters as well as its meanings in itself.

But such a fluidity of meaning is of course intolerable in allegory. Hawthorne's artistic method is to use allegory to destroy the absolute certitude of the allegorical mind: by offering several certainties which any given phenomenon, wonder, or providence may be believed to represent, and by attributing to each of these alternatives a tenable claim to absolute belief, Hawthorne undermines the dogmatic monism of allegory itself. His reliance upon the folklore of providences as well as the theological absolutes of Puritanism made available to him the resources of this 'formula of alternative possibilities,' as Yvor Winters has termed it. Its first occurrence in *The Scarlet Letter* concerns the interpretation of a wild rose which has sprouted at the threshold of the first structure erected by the Puritans in the new colony — a prison:

> This rose-bush, by a strange chance, has been kept alive in history; but whether it had merely survived out of a stern old wilderness, so

long after the fall of the gigantic pines and oaks that originally overshadowed it,—or whether, as there is fair authority for believing, it
had sprung up under the foosteps of the sainted Ann Hutchinson, as
she entered the prison-door,—we shall not take upon us to determine.

We note that the choice is unresolved between a botanical happen-
stance and a Divine providence — ironically, from the Puritan view,
linking Hester to the heretical Mrs. Hutchinson and connecting
both with a saint's legend.

This style seems indubitably Hawthorne's own. Its salient feature is the skeptical offering of the multiple meanings, each borne
aloft by the clause of a rather formal periodic sentence. The tone
of this style is curiously both detached and committed, both
amused and serious, both dubious and affirmative. Its commitment,
seriousness, and affirmation, however, all point to something other
than the literal content of its assertions; toward *that* the style
indicates detachment, amused tolerance, dubiety. What is seriously
affirmed is that *something* was signified by the rosebush. But the
very presence, uncontradicted, of both alternatives quite compro-
mises our willingness to believe unreservedly in either. Yet again,
the fact that both are possible deters us from dismissing either one.
Hawthorne uses his device of multiple choices to affirm neither the
absolute claims of Puritan dogma nor the absolute claims of right
reason. What it does affirm is, as one would expect of Hawthorne,
a multiple truth larger than either of the partial truths offered
by its alternatives: the world of fact *is* an hieroglyph of the spirit,
and the language of the spirit is beyond the capacity of either
unassisted belief or unassisted reason to read aright. Perhaps its
reading requires the collaboration of both the intellect and the
passions.

How did Hawthorne invent, or where derive, his most characteristic stylistic device? Here is another instance of the alternative
possibilities offered the reader to explain a supernatural event. The
subject of this passage is Sir William Phips, Royal Governor of
Massachusetts during the witchcraft trials in 1692, who rose to
wealth through the discovery of buried treasure:

It was reported, that he had dreamed where the galleon was laid.
Whether his extraordinary spirit of enterprise, led him to undertake
the search of the wreck, and taking advantage of the delusive spirit
of the times, he pretended to the favour of a vision which he never
had, in order to procure assistance in an undertaking which a rational

calculation might not render worthy of the hazard attending it; or whether having placed his imagination upon the scheme, his mind embraced the object in an agreeable manner when he was asleep, or whether there was a divine special influence in his favour, is not yet detached.

Hawthorne twice wrote of Phips[2] but the passage just quoted is not by him. It was published nine years before his birth in a book from which he mentions having taken the motif of 'The Great Carbuncle' (1837). The account of that Indian legend is skeptically dismissed, as a chimaera practised upon the gullible Puritans, on the page immediately preceding the account of Sir William's treasure-laden dream. James Sullivan, in his *History of the District of Maine* (Boston, 1795), reflects the rationalism of his time in the presentation of all such wonders of the invisible world. As for witchcraft, he is proud to avow that the sensible settlers of Maine had no use for that delusion which so painfully afflicted their brethren in Massachusetts. And yet for all his liberality and rationality, Sullivan cannot bring himself wholly to dismiss the possibilities of religious supernaturalism, although he is openly scornful of what he takes to be mere superstition.

I do not suggest that Hawthorne modelled his style on Sullivan's, but that the similarities in their treatment of marvels indicate a like cast of mind. Hawthorne, too, inclines toward rational skepticism; yet even more than the historian of Maine, he is unwilling to give all to reason and so deny the supernatural portent whose existence proves for him the reality of the world of spiritual truths. Indeed, in his presentation of wonders Hawthorne made them as plausible as possible, as though to emphasize the partial claims of both reason and belief. Just as he studied the wonders reported by the Puritan chroniclers, he did research too on the scientific explanations of extraordinary phenomena. In September 1837 he had borrowed Sir David Brewster's *Letters on Natural Magic* (London, 1832) from the Salem Athenaeum. This study gave explanations from the sciences of acoustics, optics, mechanics, chemistry, and medicine of such illusions as ghostly apparitions, spectral sounds, phantom ships, etc. — the very sorts of phenomena which Increase and Cotton Mather had so diligently collected from eye-witnesses a century and a half earlier. It may have been Brewster's dedication to Sir Walter Scott and his mention of Scott's

---

[2]*Works*, XII, 227-34; IV, 484-92.

Letters on Demonology and Witchcraft which led Hawthorne a week later to borrow that book, the most comprehensive and interpretive history of superstition he had read.

The final and definitive use in *The Scarlet Letter* of this treatment of the illustrious providence offers no less than four alternatives to the meaning of the most remarkable wonder in the book. The passage is so important that it must be quoted at some length; Dimmesdale has just mounted the scaffold, confessed himself Hester's love, and torn the ministerial garment from his breast.

> Most of the spectators testified to having seen, on the breast of the unhappy minister, a SCARLET LETTER — the very semblance of that worn by Hester Prynne — imprinted in the flesh. As regarded its origin, there were various explanations, all of which must necessarily have been conjectural. Some affirmed that the Reverend Mr. Dimmesdale, on the very day when Hester Prynne first wore her ignominious badge, had begun a course of penance . . . by inflicting a hideous torture on himself. Others contended that the stigma had not been produced until a long time subsequent, when old Roger Chillingworth, being a potent necromancer, had caused it to appear, through the agency of magic and poisonous drugs. Others, again — and those best able to appreciate the minister's peculiar sensibility, and the wonderful operation of his spirit upon the body,—whispered their belief, that the awful symbol was the effect of the ever active tooth of remorse, gnawing from the inmost heart outwardly, and at last manifesting Heaven's dreadful judgment by the visible presence of the letter. The reader may choose among these theories.

What is yet more remarkable, however, is the testimony of still further eye-witnesses who 'denied that there was any mark whatever on his breast, more than on a new-born infant's.' Such an infant of course is Pearl, who is everywhere equivalent to the scarlet letter itself. But before we follow that unmarked babe, let us note the interpretation of Dimmesdale's death proposed by those who saw no mark on him. They denied that he had 'even remotely implied . . . the slightest connection, on his part' to Hester's guilt.

> According to these highly respectable witnesses, the minister, conscious that he was dying,—conscious, also, that the reverence of the multitude placed him already among saints and angels,—had desired, by yielding up his breath in the arms of that fallen woman, to express to the world how utterly nugatory is the choicest of man's

own righteousness . . . He had made the manner of his death a parable, in order to impress on his admirers the mighty and mournful lesson, that, in the view of Infinite Purity, we are sinners all alike.

Now a parable is just as much an allegory as is a providence, whether the latter be the result of a wizard's black magic or Heaven's dreadful judgment. Lest we be too prone to accept this parable, Hawthorne immediately qualified the testimony of his 'highly respectable witnesses':

Without disputing a truth so momentous, we must be allowed to consider this version . . . as only an instance of that stubborn fidelity with which a man's friends . . . will sometimes uphold his character, when proofs, clear as the midday sunshine on the scarlet letter, establish him a false and sin-stained creature of the dust.

There are ironies within the ironies of Hawthorne's style; the very disclaimer of the parable of Dimmesdale's death supports the lesson which that death was said to be meant to teach.

Among all these versions, where, indeed, is the truth? We, as well as the onlookers, have been given evidence throughout the book to uphold each of the four alternatives. The final choice, however, based on the denial that Dimmesdale was either marked or guilty, is yet a deeper revelation of spiritual truth than the three which found on Dimmesdale's flesh a manifestation of his suffering spirit.

III

It is apparent that the Puritans badly bungled the case of Hester Prynne. The scarlet letter they condemned her to wear was a self-evident judgment: A for Adultery. 'Giving up her individuality, she would become the general symbol at which the preacher and moralist might point, and in which they might vivify and embody their images of woman's frailty and sinful passion.' Hester would cease to be a woman, and be henceforth a living emblem in a morality play: guilt without redemption, suffering without end.

Yet in her first appearance the child at her breast made her, 'A' and all, resemble 'the image of Divine Maternity.' By mid-point in the tale we can be told that 'The scarlet letter had not done its office,' for her 'A' has taken on significations unintended by the judges. After some years of tending the sick as a 'self-ordained

Sister of Mercy,' it was said that 'The letter was the symbol of her calling. . . . They said it meant Able, so strong was Hester Prynne, with a woman's strength.' Stranger still, it 'had the effect of the cross on a nun's bosom,' endowing Hester with 'a kind of sacredness.' Yet she herself tells Pearl that the 'A' is 'The Black Man's mark,' and when, in her forest rendezvous with Dimmesdale, she removed the scarlet letter, and shook loose her hair, she was at once transformed. 'Her sex, her youth, and the whole richness of her beauty, came back,' as sunshine flooded down in token of the sympathy of Nature — 'that wild, heathen Nature of the forest, never subjugated by human law, or illumined by higher truth.'

But now Pearl does not recognize her mother.

Many modern readers find Hester's elf-child intolerably arch, with her pranks and preternatural knowledge. She is indeed a remarkable infant, distinguished as much for her fidelity to the actual psychology of a three-year-old child as for the allegorism with which Hawthorne manipulates her strange behavior. Her fixation upon the 'A' might seem completely arbitrary, yet children of that age do indeed become attached to familiar objects in just such a fashion. Pearl was closely modelled on Hawthorne's own little daughter Una. And if Una was named for Spenser's allegorical heroine, Pearl, as Mr. Male remarks, takes her name from the passage in Matthew which signifies truth and grace.[3] When Hester strips herself of the scarlet letter she regains her pagan sexuality in the heathen world of Nature, beyond human law and divine truth. She has also taken off a token familiar to Pearl since earliest infancy. Both literally and figuratively, her child must resent her changed appearance until the familiar badge of discipline is resumed.

At one point Pearl amuses herself by mimicking her mother. She has been gazing into a pool in the woods, 'seeking a passage for herself into its [reflected] sphere of impalpable earth and unattainable sky.' Her attempt to merge herself into the elements is unavailing, and she turns to other tricks. She makes herself a mantle of seaweed, and, 'As the last touch to her mermaid's garb, Pearl took some eel-grass, and imitated, as best she could, on her own bosom . . . the letter A, — but freshly green instead of scarlet!' When Hester beholds her handiwork she says, 'My little Pearl, the green letter, on thy childish bosom, has no purport. But dost thou know, my child, what this letter means which thy mother is doomed

---

[3]Cf. 'the Pearl of Great Price' in 'The Intelligence Office,' *Work*, II, 370.

to wear?' Pearl, with her preternatural intuition, answers 'Truly do I! It is for the same reason that the minister keeps his hand over his heart!' But Hester cannot bear to tell her what she seems already to know, and breaks off, saying, 'I wear it for the sake of its gold thread.'

This scene perhaps seems a digression which fails to advance our understanding of either Hester or Pearl. But in fact it comprises a metaphoric recapitulation and explanation of the nature of Hester's offense. Pearl's allegorical function brings into *The Scarlet Letter* the pagan values which Hawthorne had synthesized in 'The Maypole at Merry Mount.' But in *The Scarlet Letter* the amoral freedom of the green natural world is viewed with yet greater reservations than was true of his story, written fifteen years earlier. We have already noticed that the forest is described, in Hester's rendezvous with Dimmesdale, as 'wild, heathen Nature.' The child will not let her mother cast the scarlet letter aside because Pearl herself is emblem of a passion which partook of that same heathen, natural wildness. 'What we did had a consecration of its own,' Hester assures Arthur, but that consecration was not a Christian or a moral sanctity. It was an acknowledgment of the life force itself. Consequently Pearl is endowed with the morally undirected energies of life. 'The spell of life went forth from her ever creative spirit, and communicated itself to a thousand objects, as a torch kindles a flame wherever it may be applied.' This spell is the power of fecundity, and its derivative power, that of imagination. 'The unlikeliest materials — a stick, a bunch of rags, a flower — were the puppets of Pearl's witchcraft . . .'[4] These she brings to life, and she feels in herself kinship with life in every form. Although the forest is a place of dread and evil, the haunt of witches and of heathen Indian sorcerers, Pearl is at home among its creatures. It 'became the playmate of the lonely infant' and 'put on the kindest of moods to welcome her.' Squirrels fling their treasured nuts to Pearl, while even wolves and foxes take caresses from her hand. 'The mother-forest, and those wild things which it nourished, all recognized a kindred wildness in the human child.'

It was in this mother-forest that Hester had had her tryst with Dimmesdale, beyond human law and divine truth. Hester herself

---

[4]Compare the passage on imagination in 'The Custom House' chapter: 'Nothing is too small or too trifling to undergo this change [from materiality into things of intellect], and acquire dignity thereby. A child's shoe; the doll . . . the hobby-horse. . . .'

sees that 'The child could not be made amenable to rules. In giving her existence, a great law had been broken; and the result was a being whose elements were perhaps beautiful and brilliant, but all in disorder.'

What is lacking in Pearl of course is the imposition of that transcendent ordering principle which man, through grace, imposes upon Nature. Lacking this, she seems to the Puritans a 'demon offspring.' Mr. Wilson, the most humane among them, asks her, 'Art thou a Christian child, ha? Dost know thy catechism? Or art thou one of those naughty elfs or fairies, whom we thought to have left behind us, with other relics of Papistry, in merry old England?' Pearl is indeed an elf, a pre-Christian Nature-spirit in human form, whose soul must be made whole by submission to divinely ordered morality before it can be saved. Mistress Hibbins, the witch, is eager to attach Pearl to her legion, and tells her that her father is the Prince of the Air, just as she tells Dimmesdale to let her know when he goes again into the forest, for 'My good word will go far towards gaining any strange gentleman a fair reception from yonder potentate you wot of.' When Dimmesdale protests that he was only on his way to greet the Apostle Eliot,

'Ha, ha, ha!' cackled the old witch-lady. . . . 'Well, well, we must needs talk thus in the daytime! You carry it off like an old hand! But at midnight, and in the forest, we shall have other talk together!'

Dilmmesdale, however, has not yet sold his soul to the devil, as had Young Goodman Brown — who was lawfully wedded at that. Dimmesdale's intuitive knowledge of the sin that sears all human hearts has made him more compassionate, not less so, and his sufferings result from his moral cowardice rather than from the presumptive sin of loving Hester. In the exposition of Dimmesdale's spiritual progress Mistress Hibbins plays a considerable role, though she remains a minor character. We find her present, for instance, on that midnight when Dimmesdale mounted the scaffold but could not bring himself publicly to confess his sin. He shrieks aloud, but no one awakes, or, if they did, 'the drowsy slumberers mistook the cry either for something frightful in a dream, or for the noises of witches . . . as they rode with Satan through the air.' Besides the family group (Hester, Pearl, and Chillingworth) there are but three observers of Dimmesdale's self-torment. One is Governor Bellingham, who comes to his window, startled by the cry. He is the surrogate of earthly power, the ranking representative of civil

government. Dimmesdale could confess to him, but he does not
do so. A second observer appears at the window of the same
house — Mistress Hibbins, who is Governor Bellingham's sister. In
historical fact one Mrs. Ann Hibbins, 'widow of one of the fore-
most men in Boston and said to have been a sister of Governor
Bellingham,' was executed for a witch in 1656.[5] This account fitted
Hawthorne's schematic purposes perfectly, to have the figurehead
of Earthly Power aligned by blood and residence with the Mistress
of Darkness. The third passerby is the Reverend Mr. Wilson, who
'came freshly from the death-chamber of Governor Winthrop.' Thus
Dimmesdale's abortive confession is made at the moment of the
reception into Heaven of a Puritan saint. Wilson represents the
power of Heavenly succour. These are the three realms of power
in Puritan New England — civil, daimonic, and divine. Dimmesdale
is thus given opportunities to ally himself with each, and allay or
compound his guilt. But his isolation is so complete that none of
these links with man, the devil, or God, can comfort him.

I would suggest that Mistress Hibbins's role as a witch should be
taken as seriously in *The Scarlet Letter* as was the use of witchcraft
in 'Young Goodman Brown.' Indeed, she brings into the moral
universe of *The Scarlet Letter* all of the associations which are so
fully developed in the earlier story. Like Young Goodman Brown,
like Mr. Hooper, like Dimmesdale himself, she, who has experienced
sin herself, has intuitive knowledge of the sinful nature of her
fellow-mortals:

> Many a church-member saw I, walking behind the music, that has
> danced in the same measure with me, when Somebody was fiddler
> . . . But this minister! Couldst thou surely tell, Hester, whether he
> was the same man that encountered thee on the forest-path?

Hester, startled, protests that she knows nothing of this. But
Mistress Hibbins takes the scarlet letter to be Hester's badge in
her own sorority of sin:

> I know thee, Hester; for I behold the token. . . . But this minister!
> Let me tell thee, in thine ear! When the Black Man sees one of his
> own servants, signed and sealed, so shy of owning to the bond as is
> the Reverend Mr. Dimmesdale, he hath a way of ordering matters
> so that the mark shall be disclosed in open daylight to the eyes of
> all the world!

---

[5]John Hale, *A Modest Inquiry into the Nature of Witchcraft* (1702), reprinted
in G. L. Burr, *Narratives of the Witchcraft Cases*, 1648-1706 (New York, 1946),
p. 410, n. 1.

Who could say that the demonic prophecy failed of fulfillment? Mistress Hibbins had already set her cap for Hester's soul. Like a good witch she is always on the look-out for acolytes, and so she had whispered 'Hist! . . . wilt thou go with us to-night? There will be a merry company in the forest; and I well-nigh promised the Black Man that comely Hester Prynne should make one.' What saved Hester from this temptation, if such it would otherwise have been to her, was Mr. Wilson's Christian charity in granting her custody of Pearl. 'Had they taken her from me, I would willingly have gone with thee into the forest, and signed my name in the Black Man's book too, and that with mine own blood,' says Hester. As long as Hester is responsible for Pearl — who represents both the emblem of her sin and, as grace, the possibility of her own redemption, she will be proof against the blandishments of the Black Man's coven.

The salvation of Pearl depends upon Dimmesdale. Until he acknowledges himself her father she can have no human patrimony, and must remain a Nature-spirit, untouched by the redemptive order that was broken in her conception. For Hawthorne, Nature is amoral but not malign. Witchcraft is not the forest's nature; it comes into being when man repudiates God and chooses Satan. The forest, having no moral will, can shelter either the spirit of the Maypole or the self-damned coven of the Prince of Air. Hence Pearl, like the Maypole mummers, is not yet damned, because unfallen; but, like them, she is not yet wholly human either. Dimmesdale's confession wrenches her first kiss for him from Pearl, and her first tears. 'As her tears fell upon her father's cheek, they were the pledge that she would grow up amid human joy and sorrow, not forever do battle with the world, but be a woman in it. Towards her mother, too, Pearl's errand as a messenger of anguish was all fulfilled.'

If Mistress Hibbens be the devil's servant, the Prince of Darkness has yet a closer liegeman in *The Scarlet Letter*. From his first appearance Roger Chillingworth is described in demonic terms. He steps forth from the forest accompanied by a heathen sachem, and later avows that he has learned more of his medical arts from 'a people well versed in the kindly properties of simples' than from the universities of Europe. Indeed, the townsfolk, who had at first welcomed him as Mr. Dimmesdale's companion and saviour, by the end of chapter IX have begun to suspect that his medicine was learned from those 'powerful enchanters' skilled 'in the black arts.' And many persons of 'sober sense and practical observation' note the change that has overtaken Chillingworth. 'Now there was something ugly and evil in his face. . . . According to the vulgar idea, the fire in his laboratory had been brought from the lower regions, and was fed with infernal fuel; and so, as might be expected, his visage was getting sooty with smoke.' Here again the superstition is offered half-mockingly; yet the image, which links Chillingworth with the base, demonic alter ego of the alchemist Aylmer in 'The Birthmark' — a monster stained with soot — is indeed appropriate to Chillingworth; like Aylmer himself, Chillingworth too is guilty of an unforgivable sin of intellect, and much less forgivably so. Hawthorne goes on to aver that 'it grew to be a widely diffused opinion, that the Reverend Arthur Dimmesdale, like many other personages of especial sanctity, in all ages of the Christian world, was haunted either by Satan himself, or Satan's emissary in the guise of old Roger Chillingworth. . . . The people looked, with an unshaken hope, to see the minister come forth out of the conflict, transfigured with the glory which he would unquestionably win.' Public opinion is now unanimous in reading Chillingworth's role aright, but at the beginning of that chapter it had concurred in seeing his presence in its obscure community in a different light: it was believed 'that Heaven had wrought an absolute miracle, by transporting an eminent Doctor of Physic, from a German university, bodily through the air, and setting him down at the door of Mr. Dimmesdale's study.' At the doctor's suggestion, Dimmesdale's friends arrange for them to lodge in the same house. Not until much later do the people recognize that their German doctor may well be a Faust. Yet in the end it is popular rumor and fireside tradition which does see the truth about Chillingworth. The force of popular belief is stronger, in the end, than even the force of religious law which branded Hester, for she long outlives the censure with which her letter was to have forever marked her. The same people who reviled her at the scaffold live to seek her counsel in their own trials.

Hawthorne rather heavily underscores Chillingworth's demonism in the eleventh chapter, calling him 'the Pitiless . . . the Unforgiving.' There it is made plain that Dimmesdale's sufferings are purgatorial, but that those of his leech have no cessation in prospect since he has broken both the natural ties that bind and the natural barriers that separate men. Chillingworth's demonism is closely associated with his metamorphic power: indeed, he is the only character in this book who holds that power. From the beginning he appears in disguise, hiding his true name and his relationship to Hester, as he will later mask his vengeful hatred of Dimmesdale. Neither the minister, on his way toward repentance, nor Hester, on hers toward stoical resignation and reintegration with society, can avail themselves of such slippery tricks. Dimmesdale's seeming purity wracks him with inward torture, while Hester is bound by Chillingworth's will, not her own, to conceal his relationship to her. The lovers' desperate plan of escaping from New England to assume new identities among the anonymous multitudes of London is stillborn, and not only because Roger would prevent it. Just as Hester realizes that she cannot flee, so is Dimmesdale drawn again and again to the scaffold, the scene of her public and his secret shame. They can struggle toward grace, they can know their own true identities, only in their own persons. And they are what their histories have made them be. But Chillingworth, like the hero of 'Wakefield,' like Ethan Brand, steps out of his place in the procession of life to try on new identities in the pursuit of the Unpardonable Sin. One would scarcely guess, from the fate of the metamorphic wizard, that the hero of Hawthorne's next romance would be a Yankee master of self-transformation.

Earl H. Rovit

Ambiguity in Hawthorne's *Scarlet Letter*

Nathaniel Hawthorne's masterpiece, *The Scarlet Letter*, presents some serious difficulties to the student of American culture who is determined to discover in that culture a unifying pattern of philosophic and aesthetic behavior. American culture is popularly regarded as being dreadfully practical, vaguely optimistic, and almost criminally naïve. *The Scarlet Letter*, however, has little traffic with the practical, less with the optimistic, and seems almost unnaïve enough to have been written by a Frenchman. As Hawthorne himself remarked — and whether this was with tongue in cheek or not we shall reserve for later consideration — his tale has "a stern and sombre aspect: too much ungladdened by genial sunshine." When we recall William Dean Howells' later strictures on American literature which suggested that American writers could not write tragedies without being false to the most essential spirit of American life — a judgement which if it has since been used as a whip with which to berate Howells is nonetheless perspicacious and valid — we have reason to look back at Hawthorne's

From *Archiv für das Studium der Neueren Sprachen und Literaturen,* CXCVIII (June 1961), 76-88. Reprinted by permission of the author.

Letter and wonder where it came from and to whom it could have been sent. For the tale does seem to be a sombre one; it is ungladdened by the kind of delightful irony which Hawthorne knew so well how to employ in his other stories. Indeed, the one novel in the nineteenth century which makes a meaningful comparison with Hawthorne's *Letter* is *Anna Karenina*, one of the novels which occasioned Howells to warn American writers away from tragedy. I do not know how Howells reconciled this sombre *Scarlet Letter* with his notion that American art can deal most successfully with 'the smiling aspects of life', but it should be recognized that this cultural problem is raised by the very existence of *The Letter*.

But this is not the only problem which *The Letter* poses. If we could pretend for a moment that the novel was written in a cultural vacuum — if we were freed from the obligation of reading *The Letter* in relationship to other American literary works, we should still be in some rather unhappy difficulties. *The Letter* is easy enough to read — so easy that it has long been a staple item in the reading curriculum of the American highschool — but its meaning is another thing.[1] We are presented with a seemingly simple enough triangle situation. The sin has been consummated, the sinners are partially exposed, and the aggrieved party to the triangle is hard at work in pursuing the still concealed guilty party. The novel moves from a kind of detective story format (who was the cad who fathered Hester's child and then let her bear the full brunt of punishment?) to a kind of pursuit-escape scenario where the reader finds himself emotionally allied to the outlaws and hostile to the avenging justice. But, of course, the novel is not that simple at all.

First, there is some dispute as to who the actual protagonist is. Many readers assume it to be Hester Prynne, sinned against more

---

[1]The interpretative study on Hawthorne's *The Scarlet Letter* is so extensive and relatively familiar that I think it unnecessary to provide thorough documentation for each critical position. The Hawthorne student will observe that I have read and profited in varying proportions from the staple items in the Hawthorne bibliography, but I should like to cite the following as being especially useful to me: Marius Bewley, *The Complex Fate* (London: 1952); Frederick I. Carpenter, 'Scarlet A Minus', *College English*, v (Jan., 1944), 173-80; Richard Harter Fogle, *Hawthorne's Fiction: The Light and The Dark* (Norman: 1952); John C. Gerber, 'Form and Content in *The Scarlet Letter'*, *New England Quarterly*, xvii (March, 1944), 25-55; Roy R. Male, *Hawthorne's Tragic Vision* (Austin, 1957); Hyatt H. Waggoner, *Hawthorne: A Critical Study* (Cambridge: 1955); Yvor Winters, *Maule's Curse* (Norfolk: 1938); Charles Feidelson: *Symbolism and American Literature* (Chicago: 1953) and Edward H. Rosenberry: *Melville and the Comic Spirit* (Cambridge: 1955).

than sinning, who bears her penance with dignity and fortitude. The difficulty with this interpretation is that one is faced by the ambiguity of her resolution. She certainly acknowledges her sin, not only socially but as an inviolable truth within her heart, and yet there is no evidence that her penitence is real. In fact, in her wilderness interview with Dimmesdale, she seems more than willing to recommit the sin and she exerts all her rather formidable powers to carry him away with her so that they can sin at their leisure and live happily ever after. Sympathize as we may with Hester's desires — and most readers do, I think — it is hard to reconcile this unrepentant Hester with the protagonist of a moral tale. In an attempt to avoid this problem, some critics have sought a different interpretation which would retain Hester as protagonist and at the same time render her capable of being evaluated in a moral frame. These critics have usually invoked some variation of the concept of the *felix culpa*, the Fortunate Fall: Hester sinned in order to ascend in humanity; her sin was a real one and her penance was even more real. In this interpretation, her lack of penitence is a testimony to her successful transcendence as a human being. Indeed, some devotees of this interpretation have become so enthusiastic as to erase the sin completely and view Hester as the incarnation of a kind of virile feminism which several generations later would result in a Susan B. Anthony or a Carrie Nation. There are some merits, of course, in this view, particularly as it opens the possibilities for exhibiting the deep roots of Hawthorne's sympathies with the Transcendentalists, but it distorts dangerously the pigments of Hawthorne's canvas which are, alas, not peach-blossom and azure, but dark greys and browns, ultimately unlivened by the single lurid flame of scarlet.

Dissatisfied with this view there has been an increasing movement in American criticism to use *The Letter* as an indication of Hawthorne's tragic vision. It is a cliché in our contemporary thinking about American literature to see this literature as possessing two threads of continuity: the light and the dark, the optimistic and the pessimistic, the naïve innocence and the shattered experience — in short, the crude ebullience of *Leaves of Grass* and the life-tempered restraint of *Moby Dick*. And since one cannot be satisfied with less than the best, the pessimistic strand had to have some tragedies to hang upon it — Howells notwithstanding — and *The Letter* became translated into an American tragedy. From this view Hester Prynne certainly wouldn't do as a tragic protagonist. She is female and, worse, a nonvirginal female in a way that

Antigone never is; she is, at least for the duration of the novel, a passive rather than an active sufferer; she is too long too honest with herself to be eligible for a recognition scene; and she rises continually through the action without any tragic *dénouement* at all. Thus the critics of this persuasion were forced to seek another protagonist and the most likely character was not terribly difficult to find. Roger Chillingworth was counted out from the very beginning and Arthur Dimmesdale was twisted into the contorted shape necessary for the new role he was to play. This interpretation focused almost entirely on the poor minister and focused beyond that on the final scaffold scene where he escapes the torture of Chillingworth and the greater tortures of his own heart for the dubious sanctuary of heaven and tragic grandeur. The case, lest I seem to be too overbearing, has been argued with cogency and even eloquence, but that it offends drastically the immediate reading experience of even the shallowest adolescent would seem to me patently obvious. He knows that Dimmesdale is basically a coward, a weakling, a pallid intellectual who uses rationalization to cover up his lack of moral courage. Indeed, Dimmesdale with all his rant and wasting away bemuses the thoughtful adolescent who has thought enough about the facts of conception and birth to wonder how Hester could ever have had the patience to submit to a seduction, or how Dimmesdale could ever have so transcended himself as to have attempted one. Even though Hawthorne strategically begins his novel after the passionate act which has set the novelistic forces into motion, it is necessary that the reader believe in the possibility of that passion in order to respond to its results. With Hester in the foreground he is never in such doubt. She is probably the one successful woman in American literature who retains her womanhood without its being disconcertingly overstressed. As long as the reader's focus is more strongly on Hester than on Dimmesdale, the passion is believable; but pushing Dimmesdale into the dominant position of the novel succeeds only in throwing into doubt the very impetus of the novel's action — surely too expensive a price to pay to make a great tragedy.

Accordingly we can see two major difficulties which *The Letter* imposes on the reader. First, the problem of reading the novel: What after all is Hawthorne driving at? What moral lesson are we to grasp from this allegorical tale? And the second — and they surely must be related — where did this sombre tale come from anyway? How can we link *The Letter* to the other American works of the period? If *The Letter* is an American masterpiece, in what sense is it American at all? As I attempt to deal with these two questions, I should point out that I do not at all presume by my tentative answers to cancel out the many other provocative and doubtless valid interpretations of *The Letter* which we are all familiar with. However, it seems to me that no interpretation of Hawthorne's major novel which does not account for its integral place in American literature can fully explain the power of the book or the delicate balance of relationships which the book successfully presents.

The key to *The Scarlet Letter* lies, I believe, in the long introduction, 'The Custom-House Sketch', which Hawthorne carefully prefixed to his story. He once explained that the reason for this long preface — it occupies almost a sixth of the complete edition — was an effort to put together enough pages to warrant the price of the book. The critic has a right to be wary of such ingenuous explanations, particularly when we remember that even after the successful publication of *The Letter* — when amplitude was no longer a question — Hawthorne insisted on the continual use of his introduction. The introduction is usually skipped over by students and teachers alike except for such general observations as might cover the autobiographical elements in the sketch, Hawthorne's description of his aesthetic, and perhaps a discussion on the unenviable situation of the American artist in the nineteenth century. However, this neglect of the introduction is, I think, ultimately perilous, because the entire work must be taken as a whole, and one of the significant elements — perhaps the most significant functional element in the novel — is the introductory sketch.

Here Hawthorne introduces the protagonist of the tale — himself — and develops ironically the major questions which the tale proper is to dramatize so effectively. Technically, as I shall try to demonstrate later, the introductory sketch is to the tale proper as would be the Ishmael chapters to the adventures of Ahab with the White Whale, if those chapters were extracted from and prefaced to the entire *Moby-Dick*. Ishmael, painfully and humorously grappling with the vast enigmas presented to him by his initiation voyage in pursuit of the Whale, is like the self-portrait of the narrator which Hawthorne presents in 'The Custom-House Sketch' as he grapples with similar problems which become explicit in the mystic evocations which stream forth from the ragged letter, 'subtly communicating themselves to his sensibilities, but evading the analysis of his mind.'

Let me in some detail recall the introductory sketch, because its neglect leads to those interpretative dead-ends which I have before mentioned. The tone of the sketch is in the most charming essay-istic prose of which Hawthorne was a master. The character of the narrator is disarmingly presented with a gentle irony that spares nothing its smile, its wry deprecation, including above all the nar-rator himself. We are all sufficiently familiar with Hawthorne's famous statements about his Puritan ancestors, those 'stern and black-browed' men who would look with disgust on their descen-dant as a mere 'writer of story books', and somewhat less with the general description of life in the Custom-House. However, a more careful reading points to one basic theme running through the introduction, one question repeated from several different angles, a theme which is incarnate finally in the tale itself.

First Hawthorne explains why and how he happened to return to his native Salem as Deputy Collector in the Custom-House. He describes the dilapidated appearance of the office as well as the once-thriving wharves of Salem, and he attempts to imagine the busy commercial days of the past when Salem was a prosperous port and the Custom-House an office of importance and enterprise. He explains that although he has no great love for Salem as such — in fact he is rather depressed by it — he has returned because his family set its roots there and he speculates on the generic line of continuity which threads between his family ancestors and his own blood and bone. Here as he offers his famous remarks on how ill they would judge him as a degenerate idler, he also judges them as fanatic iron-spirited bigots whose passions were too often ruled by a narrow and mean self-righteousness. Then he goes on to describe his associates, with one exception old men who had found a sinecure for themselves beneath the sheltering wings of the National Eagle. He marvels at these men, weathered seacaptains and superannuated military officers, the prime of whose lives had been spent in what seems to Hawthorne heroic acts of splendor and meaning. He marvels at the great gap which falls between their fullblooded experience and the torpid animality of their present lethargy. Once they fronted the full force of the winds and sea, or repulsed the enemy's charge; now their thoughts return to the past only to recall a good meal or a warm drink, and they laze in the warmth of their memories like somnolent old dogs in the sun. It is from this context that Hawthorne moves into his discussion of art and his own difficulties as an artist.

And yet there is more than a charming informal ramble around the writer's workshop in these pages. What seems to ramble actually introduces quite acutely the concern which Hawthorne is at pains to demonstrate in the novel proper which follows. These seemingly unrelated descriptions and anecdotes focus on a single theme: the relation of the past to the present — in the history of a community, in the history of a family, in the continuous pattern of one's own life. In each case there is a dramatic gap, an existential hiatus in the living chain of time which remains unsettled, unsolved in Hawthorne's mind. The Custom-House and the Salem which Hawthorne experiences intimately through the shock of his own experience have no relationship to that other Salem of fifty years before when industry and commerce thrived. What have those stern Puritan ancestors to do with the idler who writes romances? What can the broken animal lives of those old sea-captains have to do with any experience of heroism and human valor? And this Hawthorne himself, this friend of Thoreau and Emerson and even Alcott, this writer of story-books — what relationship does he have to the Hawthorne of the Custom-House, the grave meticulous inspector of revenues? These are basic questions concerning significance itself, basic questionings of the meaning of meaning, and the value of value. In the overwhelming flood of infinite events which make up the actual felt-moment of time, is there any residue from the past, any controlling germ from the moment before which carries itself along into the present, exerting its force toward pattern? If the principle of life is change, then must not life be a disintegrating flux of isolated moments strung together only by treacherous memory and sentimental nostalgia? And if this is true, then is not meaning itself meaningless? Is not the law of life sheer chaos, illusorily placed in tentative form by the indolent inertia of habit and custom? These, it seems to me, are the questions which Hawthorne asks as a preparation for his meeting with the scarlet letter — a ragged embroidered cloth which the stage business of the preliminary section of the introduction has sensitized the reader to behold.

The ragged letter becomes the repository of the question, a supposed vestige of that past upon which Hawthorne has brooded, an inheritance from his Puritan ancestors which is somehow connected with his receptive mind. The letter, meaningless in itself, a faded grotesque piece of cloth shaped to represent a capital 'A', is the perfect sign of arbitrary meaningfulness or meaninglessness; in itself it means nothing and yet it can potentially mean anything.

It is the Alpha which contains its own Omega, a protean complex which changes as man's will toward it changes. 'Life is our dictionary', wrote Emerson, but Hawthorne, who was a more cautious man, began with the first entry in that dictionary and sought to plumb its meanings, investigating in the very act the question of meaning itself. It is thus with a constant note of irony that Hawthorne introduces himself, his quest, and his tale to the reader, and before we conclude with Hawthorne that his tale is a stern and sombre one meant to serve as a chronicle of the past with the gratuitous embellishment of an ethical lesson added, we would do well to explore the possibilities that the ironic mood of the introduction may be continued in a more subtle fashion throughout the tale proper.

For the letter, 'A', over which Hawthorne broods is, as all readers have recognized, the focal point of the narrative. It is linked by imagery implicitly and explicitly both with the wild rose that blooms outside the prison-house where we first meet Hester Prynne and with the equally wild infant Pearl who is the animation of the letter itself. The letter is imprinted in lightning on the heavens during the second scaffold scene and its duplication is found on the breast of the weak Dimmesdale in his death scene. The letter is thus lucid enough in the narrative, but its meaning is as variable as the flowing stream of time which Hawthorne describes in the wilderness meeting-scene between Dimmesdale and Hester. It stands for Adulteress and Angel; it is the symbol of Atonement and Ability; it is above all the uneradicable stamp of Adam, and it is significant that only Chillingworth among the major characters — he who ends up unlinked to the magnetic chain of humanity — escapes identification with the sign. As many critics have pointed out, its meaning is largely derived from the attitudes of the people who observe it. To the Puritan villagers witnessing Hester's punishment it is a simple sign of sin. To these people for whom 'religion and law were almost identical', meaning is arbitrarily and eternally fixed and there is nothing at all ambiguous about the letter. But the scarlet letter is the initial item in the lexicon of life; it spreads its roots like the rose, it comes to a maturity like Pearl, and life rejects the external imposition of arbitrary law and religion, even as it also rejects the dogmatic diabolism of Mistress Hibbins. To the wandering Indians who admire it, it is merely a gorgeous badge; the Indians themselves are close enough to the wild unpatterned flow of nature to accept signs without demanding significations. But to the main characters the letter is the unrolling scroll of their own destinies, cumulative, selfrevealing, relentless in its capacity to develop meanings which spin inexorably into a controlling web of fate, or, as Chillingworth terms it, a 'dark necessity'. As Hawthorne suggests, '. . . the crisis flung back to them their consciousness and revealed to each heart its history and experience, as life never does, except at such breathless epochs. The soul beheld its features in the mirror of the passing moment'.

For the main characters this is the function of the letter — to be a speculum of revelation to each of his own identity. Most critics and readers quite clearly understand this, but fail to understand that for Hawthorne this is not quite the whole story. Criticism has too readily taken Dimmesdale's dying words — ('Be true. Be true. Be true. Show freely to the world if not your worst, yet some trait whereby the worst may be inferred.') to be Hawthorne's homiletic conclusion to the story. Such a conclusion would conform to the traditional interpretation of Hawthorne, the good grey romancer, the hermit, the descendant of Puritanism. They forget that Hawthorne, the only significant American writer to enlist himself in the radical experiment at Brook Farm, also wrote in this novel: 'It is remarkable that persons who speculate the most boldly often conform with the most perfect quietude to the external regulations of society.' What I mean to suggest is that this novel is at least as much about the ambiguity and perhaps impossibility of meaning, as it is about meaning itself. The three principal characters create images of themselves before the enigmatic mirroring letter, and although each accepts what he feels to be true about themselves, there is no reason to believe that either Hawthorne or the reader need share in their definitions. To illustrate let us examine the three main figures briefly.

Most readers swiftly categorize Roger Chillingworth as the Fiend, begotten out of jealousy and *Paradise Lost*, and he himself comes to share in the same judgment. And yet Chillingworth has his justifications. If Dimmesdale's definition of the Unpardonable Sin is also Hawthorne's — namely, the violation of the sanctity of another human heart — then Chillingworth is certainly unpardonably sinned against. We are told that he was in his prime, a respected scholar, when he took Hester to wife. We have no reason to believe that he ever gave her cause to break their marriage vows, and in the role of the wronged husband his jealousy and desire for revenge seem natural enough. If he becomes the Fiend incarnate, a malevolent Rappaccini experimenting with the weeds which sprout in Dimmesdale's soul, it is only because he finds a reality for himself in such a role, preening as it were in the robes of Satan before the distorting mirror of the scarlet sin. It is at least worth a speculation that his posturings are pathetically comic rather than diabolic, and one can view his vengeful pursuit as a clown's miserable ordeal toward crucifixion — without glory or victory or faith. Chillingworth is the only main figure in the story who is absolutely isolated from beginning to end. He has no human contact to the outside world from the time he enters the narrative on the margins of the marketplace throng to his final despairing end. He reads the letter as an interdiction from the human community and he resolutely carries out the command with the whole force of his will and intellect. If we find him lacking in mercy and charity, we must make the same judgment on Hester and Dimmesdale, who surely find no charity in their hearts for him in his supreme wretchedness. And if we too readily convict him of the crime of dissemblance, we might well ask how else he should have acted in his situation. In other words it seems to me that Chillingworth is the victim not of his own pride or his vengeance, but of man's most basic need to read meanings into the chaos of experience. The letter is Chillingworth's death warrant as a human being — it transforms him into the Devil — but how much more noble and absurd is his transformation than the lifelessness which he would have exhibited had he read no meaning there at all.

The letter serves a similar function for Hester and Dimmesdale, and the general ambiguity with which criticism has pursued their characterizations must testify to this fundamental problem of meaning. Whether Dimmesdale is moral weakling or tragic hero, he is what he becomes through his reading of the letter as a 'Tongue of Flame,' which stabs out of the darkness and challenges him to become himself. Like Chillingworth he is unable to accept the meaninglessness of the enigmatic symbol or the fact of his experience which it represents. His torturous struggles with meaning — whether they are the wrestlings of conscience or the heroic stumblings toward moral transcendence — are his efforts to become — even as they are the very process of his becoming — himself. A distinguished member of the community, a brilliant minister with a brilliant future, he could have ignored the challenge — accepted the fact of the letter as an isolated event in an infinite series of events — and dedicated himself to the creation of whatever image of self he desired. His incapacity to do so leads to his self-flagellation, misery, and final death on the scaffold — a victim of his self-imposed meanings.

And Hester likewise marries herself to her letter, refusing to go away from the scene of her shame, although there is nothing that could keep her there. But, and this may be because she is female, she exhibits a greater flexibility before the challenge of meaning than either her husband or her lover. Meaning is in some measure for her both ornament and transferrable label. She accepts the social fact of her sin, but it is doubtful that she confuses the biology of her sin with metaphysics. She lives under the conditioning frame of the defining letter, but she is able to distinguish between it and what it represents. Thus, all three characters, in differing degrees, pirouette in response to their individual capacities to create meanings from something which itself is without meaning. And if they are individually convinced of an absolute reality in their readings of the letter, there is no reason to believe that Hawthorne followed them in their all too-human gullibility.

What this line of thought leads to, I believe, is the suggestion that the fullest meaning of *The Scarlet Letter* may be best tapped if we shift our interpretative focus away from the areas which we would naturally tend to explore. If Hawthorne is serious in terming this 'a tale of human frailty and sorrow,' it may very well be that he is concerned with a different kind of human frailty than that of sexual temptation or guilt or pride. The more essential human frailty of the tale may be man's inevitable susceptibility to freeze the flux of experience into rigid hieroglyphics of order — to interpret a whale as the agent of malevolence in the universe, to assign arbitrary meanings to a letter and then live within the dark necessity which the design imposes.

Consider, for example, the fact of sexuality in the novel. The act of passion takes place, of course, before the novel begins, but the treatment of that sexuality throws a curious light on the material with which Hawthorne is deeply concerned. Hester is a punished, but an unredeemed sinner, and yet the fact of her nonredemption matters very little to both Hawthorne and his readers. Compare in this context Tolstoy's parallel treatment of the adultery in *Anna Karenina*. There the adultery is of cardinal importance, both in the structure and the material of the novel. In *The Letter*, on the other hand, the sexual sin is of little significance, except that this violation sets up a tidy triangle of deception and exposure. It is notable that through the course of the novel the sin itself tends to disappear from the mind of the community. The reverse is true of Tolstoy's novel, where Anna becomes increasingly with every chapter that intolerable social type, the Adulteress who refuses to be hypocritical about her actions. Hawthorne's world is really a very different one from Tolstoy's — so different that their points of view help to illuminate one another's novels. In Hawthorne's fictional world — that 'neutral territory somewhere between the real world and fairyland, where the Actual and the Imaginary may meet,' the only real substantiality is that established through the relationship of the subjective perceiver to that which he perceives. Hawthorne's world lacks society almost completely in a way that American culture has always lacked society and therefore there can be almost no narrative treatment of a social sin. Tolstoy's world is preeminently a social world and his characters interpret their identities from the revolving mirror of manners which society is constantly presenting for their reflection. Anna Karenina is ultimately crushed by her society; Hester Prynne, like most American protagonists, is her own judge and jury. And if Tolstoy's novel is greater in scope and richer in texture than Hawthorne's, the latter's treats more intensely the problematic condition of individualism for contemporary readers who live in a world where social forms have become formless, and the high price of human freedom is the everpresent risk of the thwarted growth or the disintegration of personality.

Thus if we regard the structure of *The Scarlet Letter* as a complete organic unit including the seminal 'Custom-House Sketch', the tale reads in a less stern and sombre manner than we might have first believed. The charming mockery of the introduction becomes a functional element throughout the novel, mocking even as it is charmed by the vain creative efforts of the three principal actors to crystallize their lives around a fixed meaning. If these characters did not try to impose a pattern on their lives, they would succumb to the torpor of the Death-in-life — they would be one with Hawthorne's sluggardly old seacaptains in the Custom-House. But, ironically, when they do make such a creative effort, they are trapped in the absurdity of a self-imposed design and they put to death the infinite possibilities of their individual existences. The question posed from different directions in the introduction — the meaning of meaning, the significance of experience — is resolved aesthetically in the rounded symbol of the whole. Hawthorne the ironic questioner of meaning and continuity is absorbed by Hawthorne the omnipotent creator of meaning who has wrought a self-contained universe — the world of *The Scarlet Letter* — out of the ephemeral flux of life. And in so doing he has preserved the ephemerality of phenomena, even while he has artistically established the reality of meaning. From this viewpoint the admitted ambiguity of the novel can be seen as a creative achievement of prime value, rather than the failure of vision which resorts to ambiguity in order to conceal confusion.

And further, *The Scarlet Letter* becomes the culmination of that thematic impulse which informs Hawthorne's finest short stories, *The Minister's Black Veil, Young Goodman Brown, Rappaccini's Daughter,* and *Ethan Brand.* For it is to these stories rather than to the later novels that we must turn in order to see where his most elemental power as an artist resides. In these stories the focal center of each is a masterfully complex symbol — the veil, the wilderness, the garden, and the lime-kiln. In each Hawthorne is content to set his symbol in contextual relationship and then leave it for the reader's interpretation. As successful symbols each radiates a potential range of meanings as multiform as life itself, and yet each symbol is under strict artistic control. In his later novels Hawthorne tends to become lost in the proliferation of his plots, and the narrative objectivity which his form imposed upon him diverts his focus from meaning to content. Only in *The Blithedale Romance* where he places a questioning observer within the narrative frame does he manage to grope toward a happier solution, but this effort is ultimately abortive because Hawthorne was somehow more constrained with his Miles Coverdale than he was with himself in 'The Custom-House Sketch). But *The Scarlet Letter* repeats the triumphs of his earlier stories on a broader and richer canvas. Like these it has a supreme economy and control; like these it casts a single interpretative symbol with a purity of effect which lends it great power; and greater than these, it grasps a vaster imaginative area of experience, it asks specifically questions which the others can only imply, and it answers these questions in the framing of an imperishable work of art.

Austin Warren

The Scarlet Letter: A Literary Exercise in Moral Theology

I

In structure, *The Scarlet Letter* is rather a monody, like *Wuthering Heights* (its English analogue for intensity) or *The Spoils of Poynton* (with its thematic concentration), than like the massively contrapuntal and rich Victorian novel — say *Middlemarch* or *Bleak House*. And, conducted almost entirely in dialogues between two persons, or in tableaux, with something like the Greek chorus of the commenting community, it is also much nearer to a tragedy of Racine's — *Phèdre* or *Athalie* — than to the Elizabethan drama of which the three volumed Victorian novel was the legitimate successor.

This purity of method, this structural condensation and concentration, prime virtues of *The Scarlet Letter,* disturbed, while they obsessed, its author. He regretted not being able to intersperse the

From *The Southern Review,* n.s. I (Winter 1965), 22-45, and the forthcoming book, *Connections,* by Austin Warren. (Copyright © 1970, University of Michigan Press) Reprinted by permission of the author and the University of Michigan Press.

gloom of his novel by some chapters, episodes, or passages in a lighter mode. "Keeping so close to its point as the tale does, and diversified no otherwise than by turning different sides of the same idea to the reader's mind," he wrote Fields, his publisher, would bore, disgust, or otherwise alienate the reader.

The best he could do by way of conciliating the hypothetical reader was to prefix his satirical sketch, "The Customs House" — an artistic blunder, I think. The enduring power of the book lies in its "keeping so close to its point," lies in its method: looking at the "same idea" (loose word for situation or theme) from "different sides" (loose phrase for "different points of view"), itself a loose ·phrase primarily meaning, now from the community's collective awareness, now from inside the consciousness of Pearl (chiefly to be inferred from her behavior), of Chillingworth (occasionally analysed by himself, occasionally by Hawthorne), and, centrally, by Hester and by Dimmesdale.

The first eight chapters of the novel are seen from Hester's consciousness; even though the minister appears from time to time it is in his public capacity as her "pastor"; the next four concern the minister, two of them close studies of "The Interior of a Heart"; Hester again engages the next four. The Forest chapters represent the only real meeting, the only real converse between the two, in the book. Hester then recedes; and Dimmesdale becomes the center of the last four chapters.

This is a singularly proper mode of telling the story. The two characters are joined by an act which occurred before the novel opens. They never meet again save twice, ritualistically, on the scaffold, and once, rituals dispensed with, in the Forest. Otherwise, these are tales of two isolated characters, isolated save for the attendant spirit of each — Pearl for Hester; for Dimmesdale, Chillingworth. Hester's story, as that of sin made public, must begin the novel; the telling of Dimmesdale's, as that of secret sin, must be delayed till its effects, however ambivalently interpreted, begin to show. The last chapters must present both characters to our consciousness, even though Dimmesdale recedes into something like the public figure of the early chapters, lost in his double role of preacher and dying confessor.

The composition of the novel, deeply as it stirred Hawthorne, was creatively easy, for (as he wrote Fields), "all being all in one tone, I had only to get my pitch and could then go on interminably." But this high, or deep, tragic pitch made him uncomfortable — as, I dare say, did Melville's praise of his *Mosses from an Old*

Manse, in which the new friend who was beginning to write *Moby Dick* spoke of "the blackness in Hawthorne . . . that so fixes and fascinates me," singling out from that collection "Young Goodman Brown," a piece "as deep as Dante." Hawthorne, waiving the question of his "best," preferred *The House of the Seven Gables* as "more characteristic" of him than *The Scarlet Letter,* and doubtless among his tales, too, he would have preferred the "more characteristic" to the "best." A critic may be pardoned if he prefers the "best."

And certainly *The Scarlet Letter* resumes, develops, and concentrates the themes which Hawthorne had already essayed in some of his chief and greatest short stories — "Roger Malvin's Burial," "The Minister's Black Veil," and, especially, "Young Goodman Brown" — concealment of sin, penance, and penitence; the distinction between the comparatively lighter sins of passion and the graver sins of cold blood — pride, calculated revenge, the legacy of sin in making one detect, or suspect, it in others, the effects of sin.

II

In reading Hawthorne's little masterpiece, one should be careful to distinguish the "story," "fable," or "myth" from the author's comments upon it. The commenting author — an aspect of the "omniscient author" — the later Henry James (a disciple of George Eliot in his beginnings) sought to ban: I could make, I think, a good case for the strict Jamesian construction — or for the position it banned, which would exclude James' own earlier novels as well as those of Jane Austen and E. M. Forster.

But in either case the novelist has one enviable, one "dramatic," privilege. If his characters act out their willed destiny and utter the views appropriate to their characters, the novelist (who is also a non-writer, a man whose divided self approves but in part of what his *personae* say and do) has the immunity of dissociating himself from positions which he can entertain but to which he does not, as a moral voter, wish to commit himself. In Hawthorne's time, he could (if necessary) let his latent "moral" — that of his powerfully presented "myth" — go one way while, as commentator, he safeguarded his other self by uttering, in his own person, words of warning or reproof.

What the author says through his characters cannot "legally" be quoted as his attitude; but, on the other hand, what he says as commentator must, almost equally, be regarded as not the view of his total self. As commentator, he says what he thinks he believes or what is prudential. The blessed immunity and gift, thus, is to be able to give voice to all the voices in him, not, finally, attempting to suppress some of them — not, finally, to have to pull himself together too tightly into the doctrinal consistency at which a theologian or philosopher may supposedly aim and by the relative attainment of which he may be judged.

One cannot, in this, Hawthorne's central book, take "proof-texts" out of their context. Hence, the "moral" of the novel is not contained, as a once eminent critic asserted, in Hester's avowal to her "pastor" in the pagan Forest, that "What we did had a consecration of its own" — a remark to which Dimmesdale silently assents, as, in the pagan Forest, he does to Hester's plan that they take ship for England or Europe and, by changing the place and their names, escape the ban upon unmarried lovers. Nor, since so "many morals" can be drawn from Dimmesdale's misery, are we to think that the "many morals" can be summed up in the novelist's choice from among them, "Be true! Be true! Be true!" Because there are, in Hawthorne's phrase (doubtless even for him half-ironic, half-satiric of Sunday School books and tracts), many morals, the book has no "moral." At the least, half-true — and importantly true — is Henry James' conception that it was not as a "moralist" that Hawthorne was drawn to his tales and novels of sin: "What pleased him in such subjects was their picturesqueness, their rich duskiness of color, their chiaroscuro . . . ."

Certainly his literary fascination with sin was quite as much aesthetic and psychological as moral. As Henry, brother of William, so truly says of Hawthorne, "he cared for the deeper psychology." Such comparatives as "deeper," left suspended without what they are "deeper" than, I dislike; but I can't pretend — at least in this instance — not to know what is meant: deeper than analysis of manners, deeper than consciousness, deeper than normal normality — deeper also than "univalent" judgments. Ambivalence and plurivalence are the "deeper psychology" open to the novelist even when, speaking in his own person, he too, casts a vote: I do not want to say a "decisive vote," since I doubt that, as commentator, his "view" of his own work has any more authority than that of another critic: it may even, conceivably, have less.

III

Two of the characters in *The Scarlet Letter* certainly engaged Hawthorne in his "deeper psychology," and are richly developed.

About Hester, her creator had — as he did about his other brunettes, Zenobia and Miriam — ambivalent feelings. Twice, in *The Scarlet Letter*, he compares her to that seventeenth-century feminist Anne Hutchinson, whom, in *Grandfather's Chair*, his chronicle of New England history written for children, he calls (half, or more than half, ironically) "saintly" — that is, "she who was regarded by many as saintly." "Strong" women, whether sirens, seers, or reformers, were not, in his judgment, womanly; and it follows that a woman saint, if such there be, must first be a woman.

For Hester, he provides some Catholic similitudes — the most striking in the description of her first appearance on the scaffold. "Had there been a Papist among the crowd of Puritans, he might have seen . . . an object to remind him of Divine Maternity . . ." But it would have reminded him, indeed, "only by contrast, of that sacred image of sinless motherhood, whose infant was to redeem the world. Here . . . the world was only the darker for this woman's beauty, and the more lost for the infant that she bore."

After seven years, Hester's life of charity gave her "scarlet letter the effect of the cross on a nun's breast." But Hawthorne draws back from taking the view that her life of self-abnegation might seem to entitle her to receive and him to take; for such a view would be based on Hester's Stoic decorum, not on her inner life of motive and thought. She has, to be sure, done penance, and done it with dignity — but she has done it with a *proud* dignity, for she is not penitent.

Her rich and luxuriant hair, so closely hidden by her cap, has not been cropped. And, despite the commandment, "Thou shalt not commit adultery," still, seven years after the act, she believes that what she and her lover did had "a consecration of its own." It is one of Hawthorne's most acute axioms that "persons who speculate the most boldly often conform with the most perfect quietude to the external regulations of society. The thought suffices them . . . ." And so Hester, outwardly penitent and charitable, allowed herself "a freedom of speculation which our forefathers, had they known of it, would have held to be a deadlier crime than that stigmatized by the scarlet letter." Some of these doubts and theorizings concerned the position of woman; and Hawthorne, anti-feminist that he was, says of Hester that, her heart having lost its "regular and healthy throb," she "wandered without a clew in the dark labyrinth of mind . . . ."

Hester has her femininities: her loyalty to her lover and to her child and the love of the craft ("Her Needle"). But her needle, like her mind, shows something awry. For Hawthorne bestows upon her — a kinswoman in this respect to Zenobia and Miriam — a "rich, voluptuous, Oriental characteristic." Despite her self-imposed penance of making "coarse garments for the poor" — gifts to those poor who often but revile and insult her — she allows her fancy and needleship free play in designing clothes for Pearl, her "elf-child."

More signally, she shows, in the badge of shame she herself wears — and that from her first appearance on the scaffold: a pride triumphing over her shame. This does not pass unnoticed by the women spectators at the scaffold: one remarks that the adulteress has made "a pride" out of what her judges meant for a punishment. And "at her needle," though clad in her gray robe and coarsest material, Hester still wears on her breast, "in the curiously embroidered letter, a specimen of her delicate and imaginative skill, of which the dames of a court might gladly have availed themselves . . . ."

Appropriate as it is for the pious Bostonians to think Hester a witch, Hester has not signed, with her own scarlet blood, the Devil's book. Better, from an orthodox Puritan stance, that she had done so. But she has by-passed all that. She belongs in the Forest, where, in the one recorded conversation between the Pastor and his Parishioner, she meets Dimmesdale; but she belongs in the Forest, not because it is the Devil's opposing citadel to the Town, but because she is pagan — as we might now say, because she is a "naturalist." To the Forest she belongs as does "the wild Indian." For years, she "has looked from this estranged point of view at human institutions" — human, not merely Puritan — "criticizing all — with hardly more reverence than an Indian would feel for the clerical bands" — the pre-nineteenth century equivalent of the priest's collar — "the judicial robe, the pillory, the gallows, the fireside" — the doors shut upon the sanctity of wedded and familial bliss — "or the church."

"Like the wild Indian" (Hawthorne is in no real danger of saying or thinking like the "noble savage"), Hester has not judged men by their professional vestments or their status, nor institutions by virtue of their ideal rank in the hierarchy of some philosopher like Edmund Burke.

That her judgment was thus disillusioned was both good and bad: indeed, there are two seemingly contradictory truths both of which must be asserted and maintained. One is respect for persons in their representative capacities; for church, state, and university represent, with varying degrees of adequacy, the Ideas of holiness, civic virtue, and learning. The other is a dispassionately critical judgment which distinguishes between the personal and institutional representatives of the ideas and the Ideas themselves. A third, doubtless, is the dispassionately critical judgment when particular persons and particular institutions so inadequately represent the Ideas as no longer to be sufferable — to require reform, expulsion, substitution; this is the revolutionary judgment.

The difficulty of keeping these three truths — or even the first two of them — before one's mind in steady equipoise is as difficult as it is necessary. So far as I know, Hawthorne never attempted to formulate explicitly, even in brief, what I have just said; but such a conception seems clearly implicit in his attitude and in his characterizations of Hester and Dimmesdale. Hester has been taught by shame, despair, and solitude; but, though they "had made her strong," they had "taught her much amiss."

Hester's exemplary conduct in the years which follow her first scene on the scaffold must be interpreted not as penitence but stoicism, especially, a stoical disdain for the "views" of society. She is bound to her Boston bondage partly by a kind of fatalism — not the theological kind, Calvinism, but the fatalism of being bound to the place where she "sinned" and to her lover. I have put the word sinned in quotes because Hester has not repented, not thinking that she has done anything of which she should repent. She still loves Dimmesdale, or at any event pities him, as weaker than herself; and, upon Dimmesdale's appeal to her, when (by her design and his accident) they meet in the Forest, that she advise him what to do, she is immediately purposeful and practical. Let him go into the forest among the Indians, or back to England, or to Europe. She is imperative: "Preach! Write! Act! Do anything save to lie down and die!" Chillingworth's torments have made him too "feeble to will and to do" — will soon leave him "powerless even to repent! Up, and away!" And she arranges passage to England on a ship soon to leave Boston.

After Dimmesdale's death, Hester and Pearl disappear — Pearl, "for good," Hester, for many years. Yet Hester finally returns to Boston and to her gray cottage and her gray robe and her scarlet letter, for "Here had been her sin; her sorrow; and here was yet to be her penitence." The "yet to be," ambiguous in isolation, seems, in the rest of the penultimate paragraph, to mean that at the end of her life she did repent. In part, at least, this repentance was her renunciation of her earlier fanciful hope that she might be "the destined prophetess" of a new revelation, that of a time ground for "mutual happiness" between man and woman. Here Hawthorne the myth-making creator and Hawthorne the Victorian commentator get entangled one with the other. Till the "Conclusion," the last few pages, Hester had remained, in ethics, a "naturalist," for whom "sin," in its Judaeo-Christian codification, had been a name or a convention. Now she is represented as comprehending that "no mission of divine and mysterious truth" can be entrusted to a woman "stained with sin, bowed down with shame, or even burdened with a life-long sorrow. The angel and apostle of the coming revelation must be a woman indeed, but lofty, pure and beautiful," wise "through the ethereal medium of joy." Though this future "comprehension" is assigned to Hester, it is said in the voice of Hawthorne, the commentator, the husband of Sophia.

Whether applied to Hester specifically or to the mysterious new revelation to come — reminiscent of Anne Hutchinson, Margaret Fuller, or Mother Ann Lee, the pronouncement seems falsetto. Hawthorne's "new revelation," which seems (so far as I can understand it) not very new, is certainly not feminist but feminine and familial. This is the gospel according to St. Sophia, not that of either of the St. Annes. Yet Hawthorne, I think, would allow Jesus His temptations and His sufferings: it is woman whose nature is damaged, not illuminated and enriched, by sorrow.

Hester's voluntary return to the bleak cottage and the life of good works is intelligible enough without Hawthorne's "revelation" — perhaps even without postulating her final penitence — which must mean her rejection of a naturalistic ethics, her acceptance of some kind of religious belief. Ghosts haunt the places where they died; college alumni return to the campuses where they spent, they nostalgically believe, the "happiest years of their lives"; we all have "unfinished business" which memory connects with the "old home," the town, the house, the room where we were miserable or joyful or, in some combination, both. There was a time, and there was a place, where, for whatever reason — perhaps just youth, we experienced, lived, belonged (if only by our *not belonging* — which is a kind of belonging).

Pearl, freed (like an enchanted princess) from her bondage, has married into some noble, or titled, European (not British) family, and is now a mother; but Hester is not the grandmotherly type, nor fulfilled in the role of dowager, knowing, as she does, that — whatever the state of Continental ignorance or sophisticated indulgence — her pearls are paste, her jewels, tarnished. There can be no autumnal, worldly happiness for her. Without Christian faith, she must work out, work off, her Karma — achieve her release from selfhood.

IV

Hester's conceptions were altered by her experience; Dimmesdale's were not. Unlike her — or (in different and more professional fashion) the nineteenth century agnostics Clough, Arnold, Leslie Stephen, and George Eliot — Dimmesdale was never seriously troubled by doubts concerning the dogmas of Christianity (as he understood them) and the ecclesiastical institution, the church (as he understood it). He was by temperament a "true priest": a man "with the reverential sentiment largely developed." Indeed, "In no state of society would he have been called a man of liberal views; it would always have been essential to his peace to feel the pressure of a faith about him, supporting, while it confined him within its iron framework."

Some aspects of Dimmesdale's rituals would seem to have been suggested by those of Cotton Mather, whom Barrett Wendell, in his discerning study, aptly called the "Puritan Priest." Though Mather's Diary was not published in full till 1911, striking extracts from it appeared as early as 1836 in W. B. C. Peabody's memoir. Dimmesdale's library was "rich with parchment-bound folios of the Fathers and the lore of the Rabbis and monkish erudition . . ."; and Mather (possessor of the largest private library in New England) was, as Hawthorne could see from the *Magnalia*, deeply versed in the Fathers and the Rabbis. Those aptitudes were, among the Puritan clergy, singular only in degree. But the "fastings and vigils" of Dimmesdale were, so far as I know, paralleled only by Mather's.

To fasts and vigils, Dimmesdale added flagellations, unneeded by the thrice-married Mather. Dimmesdale's sin, one of *passion* and not of *principle* or even of *purpose* — these three possible categories are Hawthorne's — had been an act committed with horrible pleasurable surprise, after which (since the sin had been of passion) the clergyman had "watched with morbid zeal and minuteness . . . each breath of emotion, and his every thought."

It is by his capacity for passion — on the assumption that passionateness is a generic human category, and hence the man capable of one passion is capable of others — that Chillingworth first feels certain that he has detected Hester's lover. Having sketched a psychosomatic theory that bodily diseases may be "but a symptom of some ailment in the spiritual part," the "leech" declares that his patient is, of all men he has known, the one in whom body and spirit are the "closest conjoined," and appeals to the clergyman to lay open any wound or trouble in his soul. Dimmesdale refuses, "passionately," and turns his eyes, "full and bright, and with a kind of fierceness," on the "leech," and then, with a "frantic gesture," rushes out of the room. Chillingworth comments on the betraying passion: "As with one passion, so with another! He hath done a wild thing erenow, this pious Master Dimmesdale, in the hot passion of his heart!"

If a common denominator between a burst of anger and a fit of lust is not immediately apparent, some sharedness there is: in both instances, reason and that persistence we call the self are made temporarily passive. A man's passions are — by contextual definition at least — *uncontrollable*; they "get the better of" the habitual self. The man "lets himself go"; is "beside himself." It is in this breakdown of habitual control that Chillingworth finds corroboration of what he suspected.

He finds more positive verification when he takes advantage of Dimmesdale's noonday nap to examine his "bosom," there finding, or thinking he finds, the *stigma* of the scarlet letter branded on the priestly flesh. In view of Hawthorne's emphasis — or, more strictly, Chillingworth's — on the close connection between soul and body in Dimmesdale, this *stigma* appears to be like (even though in reverse) the *stigmata* of Christ's wounds which some Catholic mystics have manifested.

Hawthorne turns now to other aspects of Dimmesdale's "case." Consciousness of concealed sin may, like physical deformities, make one feel that everyone is watching him. And inability to give public confession to one's sin, the fact that (through cowardice or whatever) one cannot trust his secret to anyone, may make one equally suspicious of everyone — thus deranging one's proper reliance on some gradated series of trust and confidence.

"Have a real reserve with almost everybody and have a seeming reserve with almost nobody; for it is very disagreeable to seem reserved, and very dangerous not to be so" is the counsel bitter, but not unsage, of Lord Chesterfield. Dimmesdale has a real reserve with everyone and a seeming one, too, save when his passion briefly breaks down his habitual manner. But his cautious guard, his ever vigilant consciousness of what he conceals, has made him incapable of distinguishing between friend and foe, has broken down any confidence in what he might otherwise properly have relied upon, his intuitions. Dimly perceiving that some evil influence is in range of him, and feeling even doubt, fear, sometimes horror and hatred at the sight of the old leech, he yet, knowing no rational reason for such feelings, distrusts the warnings of his deep antipathy.

And now we come to what doubtless most engaged Hawthorne's interest in Dimmesdale: the ambivalence. Dimmesdale's sin and suffering had, in their way, educated the pastor and the preacher. Without his sin of passion and his sin of concealment, Dimmesdale would have been a man learned in books and the abstractions of theology but ignorant of "life," naive, unself-knowing. It was the self-education forced upon him by his sin which made him the pastor, the "confessor," the preacher he is plausibly represented as becoming.

At the end of his seven years, Dimmesdale is a great — or as the American vulgate would have it, "an emminently successful" — pastor and preacher. Hawthorne characterizes the categories into which his fellow-clergymen could be put. Some were greater scholars; some were "of a sturdier texture of mind than his, and endowed with a far greater share of shrewd, hard, iron, or granite understanding" (the preceding epithets show the noun to be used in the Coleridgean, the disparaging, sense); others, really saintly, lacked the Pentecostal gift of speaking "the heart's native language," of expressing "the highest truths through the medium of familiar words and images."

To the last of these categories Dimmesdale might, save for his "crime of anguish," have belonged. This burden kept him "on a level with the lowest," gave him his universal sympathies with the sinful and his sad eloqence, sometimes terrifying, but oftenest persuasive and tender. These sermons made him loved and venerated; but their preacher knew well what made them powerful, and he was confronted with the old dilemma of means and ends.

In the pulpit, Dimmesdale repeatedly intends to make a confession, and repeatedly he does; but it is a "vague," a ritual confession — like that of the General Confession at Anglican Matins, except that "miserable sinner" in whom there is no health is violently intensified by a consistently Calvinist doctrine of total depravity. No difference: Calvinist and Wesleyan and revivalist accusations against the total self can, with equal ease, become ritual. Dimmesdale never specifically confesses to adultery, only to total depravity: "subtle, but remorseful hypocrite," he knows how the congregation will take his rhetorical self-flagellation — as but the greater evidence of his sanctity; for the more saintly a man, the more conscious he is of even the most venial sins.

So the clergyman was fixed in his plight. At home, in his study, he practiced not only his physical act of penance, his self-scourging; but he practiced also a "constant introspection," which tortured without purifying. To what profit this penance unpreceded by penitence, this torturing introspection which led to no resolution, no action?

As he later told Lowell, Hawthorne had thought of having Dimmesdale confess to a Catholic priest (presumably some wandering French Jesuit) as he did, indeed, have Hilda confess to a priest in St. Peter's, not her sin (for she was "sinless") but her complicity by witness to a sin and a crime. Such an idea might have crossed the mind of a Protestant "priest" of Dimmesdale's monkish erudition and practices. But, had he acted upon the impulse, and had the Catholic been willing to hear the confession, there could have been no absolution, either sacramental or moral. Dimmesdale would have had to do real penance, make real restitution, make public confession in unequivocal terms not of his general sinfulness but of his specific sin, the committing of adultery, and of that deeper, more spiritual, sin in which he had persisted for seven years, that of concealing the truth.

What has kept Dimmesdale from confession? Hester has herself been partly at fault, has made a serious error in judgment. At the beginning of the novel, Dimmesdale, her pastor, has, in his public capacity, enjoined her to speak. His injunction that she name her child's father reads ironically as one returns to it after the "seven years" which follow. "Be not silent from any mistaken pity and tenderness for him; for, believe me, Hester, though he were to step down from a high place, and stand there beside thee, on thy pedestal of shame, yet better were it so, than to hide a guilty heart through life. What can the silence do for him, except it tempt him — yea, compel him, as it were — to add hypocrisy to sin? . . . Take heed how thou deniest to him — who, perchance, hath not the courage to grasp it for himself — the bitter, but wholesome, cup that is now presented to thy lips!"

Already Dimmesdale had, perhaps, begun to master the art he showed in his later sermons — that of speaking the truth about himself while to others (Hester excluded) he seemed to be uttering a generalization. Arthur Dimmesdale is, "perchance," a coward, weak beside Hester, whose feeling towards him, never contemptuous, partakes certainly of the maternal. Would, she says "that I might endure his agony as well as mine."

If not with all men, with some — perhaps with most, the longer confession is delayed and that, without which confession would scarcely avail — the utmost reparation, restitution, change, conversion, the more difficult it becomes. One "rationalizes" the procrastination — even though the "rationalization" never really satisfies the "rationalizer."

Dimmesdale, as we see him seven years after, appears to offer his basic rationalization in his speech to Chillingworth — expressed (like his injunction to Hester in the third chapter) in generalized, in hypothetical, terms: there are guilty men who, "retaining, nevertheless, a zeal for God's glory and man's welfare, they shrink from displaying themselves black and filthy in the view of men; because, thenceforward, no good can be achieved by them; no evil of the past be redeemed by better services."

There is some truth in what he says. It is a truth known to those who have a jail sentence on their records — or a period of mental illness. And the Catholic Church, which consistently holds that the unworthiness of a priest does not invalidate the sacraments he administers, which conducts its confessions in confessional boxes, not in the presence of a congregation, sees the degree of truth in Dimmesdale's position.

But, for all his Puritan priestliness, Dimmesdale is a Protestant; and the Catholic half-truth — if that is what we should call it — is not for him to appropriate. It is given to Chillingworth to utter the "Protestant" truth. If men of secret sin "seek to glory God, let them not lift heavenward their unclean hands! If they would serve their fellow-men, let them do it by constraining them to penitential self-abasement!"

After her interview with her pastor on the midnight scaffold, Hester is shocked to reflect upon his state. "His nerve seemed absolutely destroyed. His moral force was abased into more than childish weakness." She reflects on her responsibility. Whether Hester's or Hawthorne's — two of her reflections appear to be intended as those of both — the commentator phrasing what Hester feels: "Here was the iron link of mutual crime, which neither he nor she could break. Like all other ties, it brought along with it its obligations." She must disclose to him Chillingworth's identity; must shield her lover.

So Hester assumes her maternal responsibility to her pastor and lover. In "The Pastor and his Parishioner" the roles are ironically reversed. The two meet in the "dim wood," "each a ghost, and awe-stricken at the other ghost." One chill hand touches another almost as chill; yet the grasp of the chill and the chill took away the penultimate chill of isolation which had separated them from all mankind. Their conversation "went onward, not boldly, but step by step . . . ." They "needed something slight and casual to run before and throw open the doors of intercourse, so that their real thoughts might be led across the threshold."

Their first "real thoughts" to find expression are the mutual questions — "Hast thou found peace?" Neither has. Hester tries to reassure Dimmesdale by taking the line, the pragmatic line, which the pastor has already used, in rationalized self-defense, to Chillingworth. He is not comforted. "Of penance I have had enough. Of penitence there has been none!"

Hester sees him, whom she "still so passionately" loves, as on the verge of madness. She addresses him as "Arthur"; throws her arms around him. He is at first violent, with all that "violence of passion" which gave Chillingworth his key. Then he relents: "I freely forgive you now. May God forgive us both!" But he goes on to extenuate his sin by comparison with Chillingworth's: "We are not, Hester, the worst sinners in the world. There is one worse than even the polluted priest! That old man's revenge has been blacker than my sin. He has violated in cold blood the sanctity of a human heart. Thou and I, Hester, never did so!"

Then follow the famous words of Hester. The lovers, like Dante's yet more illustrious couple, had acted in hot blood, not in cold. And — "What we did had a consecration of its own. We felt it so! We said so to each other! Hast thou forgotten it?"

Dimmesdale replies, "Hush, Hester! . . . No; I have not forgotten!" That Hester had said so is credible. It is difficult to credit the "priest's" using any such sacred word as "consecration," though Hester remembers the word as used by both; and Dimmesdale — though his "Hush" presumably implies that he in some way now thinks it wrong — does not contradict her recollection.

Now he appeals to Hester to rid him of Chillingworth and what Hester calls the "evil eye": "Think for me, Hester! Thou art strong. Resolve for me! Advise me what to do." And Hester accepts the responsibility. She fixes "her deep eyes" on her lover, "instinctively exercising a magnetic power" over his spirit, now "so shattered and subdued . . . ."

Dismissing Dimmesdale's talk about the Judgment of God, Hester immediately — like a sensible nineteenth century physician or practical nurse — recommends a change of scene, an escape from an oppressive situation, and begins to outline alternate "tours." At first she speaks as though her lover (or former lover — one does not know which to call him) might escape alone: into the Forest to become, like the Apostle Eliot, his recent host, a preacher to the Redmen; or across the sea — to England, Germany, France, or Italy. How, exactly, a Calvinist clergyman, is to earn his living in Catholic France and Italy is not clear; but Hester seems to have unbounded faith in her lover's intellectual abilities and personal power, once he has shrugged off New England: and seems to think of his creed — and even of his profession — as historical accidents. These Calvinists, these "iron men, and their opinions" seem to her emancipated mind to have kept Arthur's "better part in bondage too long already!" He is to change his name, and, once in Europe, become "a scholar and a sage among the wisest and the most renowned of the cultivated world." He is bidden, "Preach! Write! Act! Do anything save to lie down and die!"

In all this appeal, Hester seems projecting her own energy into Dimmesdale and, what is more, seems to show little understanding of her lover's nature: could he, eight years ago, have been a man to whom changing your name, changing your creed, changing your profession could have been thus lightly considered? Can Dimmesdale ever have been a man of action in the more or less opportunist sense of which Hester sees him capable? If so, as an Oxford man (Hawthorne should have made him, as a Puritan, a Cantabrigian), he could have submitted to Archbishop Laud instead of coming to New England. What positive action do we know him to have committed in "cold blood" save that? He committed a sin in hot blood once — it is tempting to say "once," and I often think (unfairly perhaps) that Hester seduced him. Otherwise his sins have been negative and passive — cowardice and its *species*, hypocrisy.

False in its reading of his character and rashly over-sanguine of programs as Hester's exhortation may be, Dimmesdale is temporarily aroused by her strength, by her belief that a man can forget his past, dismiss its "mistakes" and "debts," and start again as though nothing had happened, as though one had neither memory nor conscience. For a moment he belives he can start all over again, if only, invalid that he is, he had not to start alone. But Hester tells him that he will not go alone: her boldness speaks out "what he vaguely hinted at but dared not speak."

Hester and Arthur part, but not before she had made plans for passage on a vessel about to sail for Bristol. When the priest learns that it will probably be on the fourth day from the present, he remarks, but to himself, not to Hester, on the fortunate timing.

It is "fortunate" because three days hence Dimmesdale is to preach the Election Sermon, the highest civic honor a clergyman could receive. That Dimmesdale should still care, should still look to this ending of his career as a dramatic close, that he should still think of his public duty more than of his private morality shocks Hawthorne as, of all Dimmesdale's doings and not-doings the most "pitiably weak." What is it, finally, but professional vanity? "No man, for any considerable period can wear one face to himself, and another to the multitude, without finally getting bewildered as to which may be the true."

The minister walks home from the Forest "in a maze," confused, amazed. Hester's bold suggestions have temporarily released him from that iron framework which both confines and supports him. His habitual distinctions between right and wrong have broken down; and all that survives is his sense of decorum.

"At every step he was incited to do some strange, wild, wicked thing or other, with a sense that it would be at once involuntary and intentional; in spite of himself, yet growing out of a profounder self than that which opposed the impulse — "profounder" in a sense Hawthorne does not define. It may be man's subconscious or his "total depravity" left to himself — the Dark Forest in man, the Satanic.

All of his impulses are rebellions against his habitual mode of life and even, one would say, of thought and feeling. Meeting one of his elderly deacons, he has the impulse to utter "certain blasphemous suggestions that rose in his mind respecting the communion supper." And, encountering the oldest woman of his church, pious and deaf and mostly concerned with recollecting her "dear departed," he can think of no comforting text from Scripture but only what then seemed to him an "unanswerable argument against the immortality of the soul," which, happily, she is too deaf to hear. To a pious young girl, he is tempted to give "a wicked look" and say one evil word, and averts the temptation only by rudeness, and to some children, just begun to talk, he wants to teach "some very wicked words." Lastly, meeting a drunken seaman from the ship on which he plans to sail, he longs to give himself with the abandoned wretch — no member of his congregation —

the pleasure of "a few improper jests" and a volley of good round oaths; and not his virtue but his "natural good taste" and still more his "habit of clerical decorum" dissuade him.

These temptations exhibit a Dimmesdale I should not have guessed to exist even in unvoiced capacity — and for which Hawthorne has given no preparation: indeed, we are never given any account of the pastor's pre-history at all comparable to that which is furnished for Hester. "The Minister in a Maze" is, indeed, something of a brilliant sketch, a "set piece" — something which occurred to Hawthorne as he was writing his novel, yet not wholly of it. Was the pastor once a young rake that he should know such "wicked words," round oaths, and smutty stories? It is highly unlikely. Intellectual doubts can occur to the most naturally religious of men; and a good man — as well as a man of taste — may hear many words which his principles and his taste would forbid him to use.

Chiefly, I shall have to defend this brilliant chapter on psychological considerations more general than specifically relevant to Hawthorne's protagonist. In the benign phenomenon called "conversion" the selves of a divided self reorder themselves: the self which was dominant is exorcised, or at any event decisively subordinated; the self which existed as subordinate — the "good self" — becomes supreme, or nearly supreme. And there is a corresponding shift of positions which we may call perversion. Both of these changes can, with certain types of men, occur — or show themselves — in a moment. Some of these reorganizations persist; some are brief, impelled as they oftenest appear to be, by the "magnetism" of an emotionally powerful propagandist — such a one as Hester.

In yielding to Hester's proposals of escape, Dimmesdale, says Hawthorne, had, in effect, made such a bargain with Satan as the witch-lady, Mistress Hibbins, suspected him of. "Tempted by a dream of happiness, he has yielded himself with deliberate choice, as he had never done before, to what he knew was deadly sin." This he now has done. Hester, out of one — "humanly speaking" — generous impulse, spared identifying Chillingworth to her lover and *concealed* her lover's name from Chillingworth, and now out of another "generous" impulse she had bade her lover to escape his concealed sin not by now exhibiting himself but by escape from his adopted country, his profession, even his name. And what have been the results of these "generous" impulses — not wholly distinterested, perhaps, since she thinks of being reunited to her lover? What have been the results of these attempts twentieth century Americans understand so well — attempts to help by sparing those we love, or think we love?

Dimmesdale returns to his study, conscious that his old self had gone. The man who returned from the Forest was wiser — wiser about himself, than the man who entered it. But — like Donatello's what a "bitter kind of knowledge." He throws the already written pages of his sermon into the fire, and, after having eaten "ravenously," he writes all night on another.

What, the attentive reader speculates, is the difference between the unfinished sermon written before the Forest and the finished one of the night that followed? That difference, like the nature of the sermon delivered, seems curiously irrelevant to Hawthorne. We are told that the new discourse was written "with such an impulsive flow of thought and emotion" that its writer "fancied himself inspired." Which is the word to be stressed: *fancied* or *inspired?* We are told that he wrote with "earnest haste and ecstasy": where is the stress? Had he something to say in the sermon which was the result of his intention (premeditated at some time before he delivered the sermon) of thereafter taking his stand beside Hester on the Scaffold? Did the sermon have some new tone in it, some tragic or bitter wisdom delivered from that gross lapse into illusion which so bemused and amazed him as he returned from the Forest?

Melville once wrote a masterly and prophetic sermon for Father Mapple. Hawthorne writes none for Dimmesdale. During the delivery of the sermon, we — with Hester — are outside the meeting house. We but hear the preacher's voice, one with great range of pitch, power, and mood. Yet, says Hawthorne, if an auditor listened "intently, and for the purpose," he would always have heard throughout the "cry of pain," the cry of a human heart "telling its secret, whether of guilt or sorrow. . . ." In this respect, however, the present sermon was not unique; for it had always been "this profound and continual undercurrent that gave the clergyman his most appropriate power."

When, after the sermon, we hear dimly from the admiring congregation, its burden, we discover in it — strange to say — that it had ended with a prophetic strain in which, unlike those of the Jewish seers, not denunciation of their country's sins, but foresight of his New England's "high and glorious destiny" had been the theme. I am at a loss to interpret this. That the preacher, about to declare himself an avowed sinner, cannot (like Cotton Mather) denounce his New England's sins, I can see; but why need he celebrate its high destiny? It would appear that Hawthorne, to whom the "subject matter" of the sermon does not seem to matter, has inserted and asserted his own strong regional loyalties!

But I dwell overlong on what, though it ought to matter to the constructor of so closely constructed a novel, seems not to have mattered to Hawthorne. What matters to him, and upon which he is utterly harsh, is that, seeing the error of escape, Dimmesdale has planned first to give the sermon, thus triumphantly ending his professional career, and then to make his public confession. The giving of the sermon as such, and the content of the sermon, don't really concern him — unless the giving of the sermon contributes the publicity and the drama of the Scaffold confession requisite to counterpart the publicity and the drama of that first scaffold on which Hester stood — save for her baby on her arm — alone.

Implied is some final clash of wills and "philosophies" between Hester and Arthur. Dimmesdale bids Pearl and Hester towards the Scaffold. Pearl, bird-like, flies and puts her arms around his knees; but Hester comes slowly, "as if impelled by fate and against her strongest will," and pauses before she reaches him. Only when Chillingworth attempts to stop the pastor's public confession and the pastor again appeals does Hester come. But Dimmesdale has assumed the man's role at last — or *a* man's role: he asks Hester for her physical strength to help him onto the Scaffold, but in asking her strength enjoins, "let it be guided by the will which God hath granted me." When they stand together, he murmurs to Hester, "Is not this better than what we dreamed of in the Forest?" Hester cannot assent. She palliates with "I know not"; then adds what seems to mean "better, perhaps, if we two and little Pearl can die together." But that, though human, is melodramatic. Hester must see that her lover is dying and that there is no way save a supernatural intervention, an "act of God," as insurance companies put it, which can kill her and the child concurrently with him.

After his confession to his parish and the revelation of his *stigma*, he says farewell to Hester. She speaks of their having "ransomed one another" by their consequent miseries, speaks of spending their "immortal life" together. He replies, as he did to her words in the Forest about the private "consecration" of their adulterous union. "Hush, Hester . . . The law we broke! — the sin here so awfully revealed — let these alone be in thy thoughts! I fear! I fear!" What he fears is not for his own salvation, assured, to his perception, apparently, by this, his deathbed repentance and confession — but for any reunion of the lovers after death.

V

It seems, to so close a reading as I have given to Dimmesdale, a pity that Hawthorne's "deeper psychology" and his own commentary, stop at this point. What is one to think of deathbed repentances, and of repentances so dramatic as this? And wasn't the repentance, if repentance there was and not yet another form of proud illusion, finally produced not by Chillingworth's malign sleuthing but Hester's "generous" and — in view of her lover's theology and character, if not indeed judged by any kind of absolute ethic — immoral advice that he escape from the consequences of his deed?

These are questions partly casuistical, partly universal, all of which one would judge to have interested Hawthorne. That they are not "worked" out is partly, perhaps, Hawthorne's judgment that from earlier comments might be inferred the comments here relevant; partly, I think, a felt conflict between aesthetic and ethico-psychological considerations: aesthetically, he wants a firm, dramatic finale — something at all times difficult for him to manage, and here one which must be reconciled as best he can with his ethically psychological concerns, his probings and questionings.

Lastly, his "conclusion" must give the modes of interpretation which the community apply to the phenomenon of the *stigma* which "most," though not all, of the spectators testified to having seen when the dying "priest" bared his breast. Even more than in his later Romances, Hawthorne sees life from inside the consciousness of a few persons — those of an introspective and meditative turn; but these persons, however insulated, are not solipsists: they believe, as Hawthorne believes, in a world they have not created by their own consciousness but merely — though that seems a meager adverb — interpreted.

The community forms, in terms of literary tradition, a Greek chorus, to the happenings in his protagonists' inner lives. Like the utterances in the choruses of, say, Sophocles, it doesn't provide what a novice enamoured of classical antiquity expects — the voice of true wisdom, the sure guide by which to interpret the too intense, and hence probably aberrative, views of the protagonists. When such a novice reads Arnold's famous praise of Sophocles that he "saw life steadily and saw it whole," the novice looks to the chorus to give that steady and whole interpretation. But the expectation is vain: the chorus partly comments, half emphatically, on what goes forward at the center of the stage, partly utters traditional maxims and apothegms which are too general.

In Hawthorne's choruses the same is true. In *The Scarlet Letter*, there are many auctorial comments on the community — comments frequently not limited to that seventeenth century Puritan community in which Arthur and Hester lived. It is impossible to reduce them to any unitary and propositional form. Hawthorne is no Utopian, whether of the Brook Farm or any other variety; he is equally free from any extravagant individualism, even of the Emersonian variety: I say "Emersonian" because Emerson himself was no such individualist as the half-gifted, half-eccentric people who appealed to his ears and sheltered themselves under his name.

Hawthorne's "community" — or "society" — is now kind, now persecuting; now foolish, now wise. Perhaps his most characteristic view of it is that, given time enough, "the people" will show wisdom and do justice. *Given time enough*, it will forget initial suspicions and hostilities — do justice to the relatively heroic individualists — Edwards, Emerson, Thoreau, Garrison, Anne Hutchinson, Eleanor Roosevelt. What if it has not time?

The relation between individual truth (that of existential insight) and the community's slowly shifting "wisdom" can never be either perfectly or permanently adjusted. Seneca wrote, "As often as I have been among men, I returned home less a man than I was before." But Aristotle opens his *Politics* with the maxim that "A man who can live alone must be either a god or a beast." *Society and Solitude* (the title of Emerson's last collection of essays) names two resorts, the two forces which must ever be "checking" and "balancing" each other.

Hawthorne's "absolute truth" and "ultimate reality" are not to be identified with any of their adumbrations. They are not imparted in their wholeness to Dimmesdale, or Hester, or to the chorus of the community, nor to Hawthorne as commentator on his own myth, nor to the author of this essay. We all know in part, and prohesy but in part. Generalizations without case histories are commonplaces; case histories without the attempt at formulating "first principles" are but (in the pejorative sense) casuistries.

This dialetical nature of truth-finding and truth-reporting Hawthorne was too honest to evade; it is to his literary as well as his "philosophical" credit.